CW00855586

STEPPING INTO
THE LIGHT

A GUIDE TO CLEARING LIMITING CORE BELIEFS

MAYLINE ROBERTSON AND NICOLE BIONDICH

BALBOA.PRESS
A DIVISION OF HAY HOUSE

Copyright © 2021 Mayline Robertson and Nicole Biondich.

All rights reserved. No part of this book may be used or reproduced by any means, graphic, electronic, or mechanical, including photocopying, recording, taping or by any information storage retrieval system without the written permission of the author except in the case of brief quotations embodied in critical articles and reviews.

Balboa Press books may be ordered through booksellers or by contacting:

Balboa Press
A Division of Hay House
1663 Liberty Drive
Bloomington, IN 47403
www.balboapress.com
844-682-1282

Because of the dynamic nature of the Internet, any web addresses or links contained in this book may have changed since publication and may no longer be valid. The views expressed in this work are solely those of the author and do not necessarily reflect the views of the publisher, and the publisher hereby disclaims any responsibility for them.

The author of this book does not dispense medical advice or prescribe the use of any technique as a form of treatment for physical, emotional, or medical problems without the advice of a physician, either directly or indirectly. The intent of the author is only to offer information of a general nature to help you in your quest for emotional and spiritual well-being. In the event you use any of the information in this book for yourself, which is your constitutional right, the author and the publisher assume no responsibility for your actions.

Any people depicted in stock imagery provided by Getty Images are models, and such images are being used for illustrative purposes only.
Certain stock imagery © Getty Images.

Print information available on the last page.

ISBN: 978-1-9822-7050-6 (sc)
ISBN: 978-1-9822-7052-0 (hc)
ISBN: 978-1-9822-7051-3 (e)

Library of Congress Control Number: 2021912612

Balboa Press rev. date: 07/16/2021

CONTENTS

ACKNOWLEDGING OUR GRATITUDE

This book is dedicated to each other. The work we put into this book went far beyond the writing, it really shined a light onto the places we needed to heal. We helped each other become better versions of ourselves through this labor of love. Every chapter revealed new ways we needed to grow. All the moments of discomfort, frustration, and heaviness paved the way for others to follow, and that has made it all worth it.

We want to thank our families and treasured friends for supporting us on our journey towards creating this book. We are especially grateful to our editor Barbra Rodriguez, Nicole's husband, Michael Swavely and our friends Ceci Norman, Lyn Vanderjagt, Holly Harris, Karen Hergett, Ellen Wilson, Shelby Yarbrough, Lindsay Moss, Courtney Folloder, Lynne Wedul, and Brea Macarov for helping to shape this workbook and for the continual inspiration you are in our lives. May we all continue to transform into the light of who we really are.

WHY IT MATTERS TO CLEAR LIMITING BELIEFS

It's a good bet that there are some challenging circumstances in your life right now. Maybe you are facing questions about God and your faith, or even faith in yourself. Maybe you're in conflict over forgiveness with your partner about something they did, or you've been wanting to open yourself up to the possibility of a love interest. You deserve to have the basic energetic tools that will heal your mind, body and every part of your life, no matter how difficult it has been so far. Perhaps you don't know your purpose or understand what direction your life should take. Whether your concerns seem large or small at the moment, we have found that limiting core beliefs of all sizes have an impact on you and your life.

We all stand in the way of our own success and growth, often without realizing it. You likely wrestle with some "could haves" and "should haves" about things you might have done differently in your life. Left unaddressed, that inner struggle is exactly what keeps you from moving ahead. Instead you stew in the darkness of not knowing what's in your way, waiting for someday to come along and rescue you. Someday when I accomplish this or that, then I will be happy. Someday when the kids are older or when I retire, then I will do something for myself.

The trouble with someday is that it never comes. All you're left with, if you don't pay closer attention, is a sense of doubt, regret or anxiety that continues to obstruct you from moving toward your dreams. The good news is you can develop ways to address the blocks that have often subconsciously fallen onto your path. While some healing practitioners focus on clearing trapped emotions related to such blocks, we show you how to dig deeper to get at the core of all your pain. The belief work we share in this workbook is a way to eliminate the limiting thought patterns and the thousands of excuses we all make for not living the life we really want.

Feeling that you need to have a more fulfilling life is likely the reason you picked up this book. You want to find a better way. The good news is, in connecting with your history of beliefs through this workbook, you will also discover your authentic self.

This clearing work that removes old, outdated beliefs about yourself and the world is like doing major spring cleaning for your heart and soul! No dust bunny or hidden creepy crawly will be safe. Every corner of your life will have the curtains thrown open and the sun shining in. You will hurt at times from using your mental and energetic "muscles" in a brand new way. Tears may come and you may feel overwhelmed for a while when you realize you have held onto so much pain. Nonetheless, you will gain so much vitality when you throw away what you have outgrown and let the unique way that you are meant to be in the world begin to emerge.

Belief work matters because you deserve to be free from someday and to live a life that is worth waking up for today! Belief work is that powerful and transforming.

How to use this workbook

This workbook explains how limiting beliefs are keeping you stuck and how you developed them in the first place. We also provide quick methods for uncovering and clearing outdated beliefs that are easy to build into your daily life. It won't take long for you to see how simple it is to heal the wounds surrounding every area of life you wish to make better. Each chapter that addresses limiting core beliefs helps you heal at a deeper level than you ever thought possible.

Here's how it works: in chapter three, "Methods to the Madness," you'll learn ways to connect to your Higher Self and tap into your own healing abilities, bringing forth what is unconscious so your conscious mind can address it. The concept you use to connect to the knowledge that transcends your mind is highly personal, and we encourage you to use whatever feels right, such as God or Higher Self.

The remaining chapters describe uncovering the layers of limiting beliefs surrounding the areas of life we have found are at the core of what most people struggle with. We also share in these chapters about clearing particular core beliefs surrounding every area of our lives.

The focus in this workbook is on removing limiting core beliefs related to:

God and Religion
Separation and Suffering
Unworthiness, Failure and Fear
Control, Worry and Doubt
Guilt, Blame and Shame
Hate, Judgment and Denial
Forgiveness and Love
Acceptance, Change and Destiny
Allowing and Trust

Faith and Certainty

Surrendering and Releasing

Considerable care has been taken to include beliefs in this first workbook that are truly at the core of what keeps everyone in pain and from moving forward in freedom. Your money problems or relationship issues cannot be healed until you get at their root cause. The underlying challenge always relates to the limiting core beliefs found in these pages.

As you work through each section of beliefs, choose whatever clearing method from chapter three that seems right for you. You will notice that some beliefs will be written in a number of different ways that ultimately mean the same thing. Why all the repetition? The answer partly reflects the mind's habit of "layering" life experience information. When you slice open an onion, you immediately notice different large layers. Less noticeable are thin membranes that separate these layers. Just as each part of an onion makes up the whole, the same is true of the layers that combine to form beliefs that limit us or that help us.

Suppose your belief is, "I am not supported by God." You may have held that belief since childhood, with variations on this isolating driver of your behavior added over time. Another belief layer might be, "God does not support me." and another, "I cannot allow myself to be supported by God and family," and "I have to do it all myself." Yet another might be "I'm not worthy enough to be supported by God." It is important to work through the layers in order to bring the entire energy of a particular belief into the light to remove it.

After working through a chapter of limiting beliefs to address those that tweak you, take some time to solidify what you have learned by using the final journaling sections and answering the prompts. Journaling is a great way to retain new information, and you can see just how much you have grown when you go back and read what you have written.

Reading this book and developing a daily practice of clearing limiting beliefs will help you become more aware of your thoughts and how tightly they are ruled by past limiting beliefs. Whatever challenges are most central in your life, you can start clearing beliefs described in that chapter (the order of the clearing work doesn't matter, although we indicate a few things to clear first to help the process overall). All that is needed is for you to make a little time for yourself to focus on this form of development.

No matter your life circumstances, you will find tools in this book that you can apply. Doing so is about finding your truth your purpose in living your truth while experiencing a deeper understanding of yourself and heightened awareness of your thoughts.

Frequencies in the midst of our beliefs

While developing the lists of limiting core beliefs in this book, we carefully considered the frequency of words in each belief statement. Each word vibrates at a particular frequency. Positive words tend to vibrate at a higher frequency where negative words have a lower vibration. This is why you will see some beliefs that have been restated, changing only one word. You can decide which belief statements feel like the right one, using one of the testing methods discussed.

What do we mean by frequency of words? Quantum physics states that all matter is energy. For the purposes of this workbook, that energy includes your thoughts, as well as beliefs lodged in your subconscious mind (a process we will explain in the next chapter).

All matter, including thoughts, beliefs, ideas and words, vibrate at different frequencies. We have found that the higher the frequency of your thoughts, the higher the quality of the experiences that will be drawn to you. How do you get thoughts of a higher frequency? By improving the quality of the beliefs you hold and of the words you speak. So we selected limiting belief statements that were of low energetic frequency, as well as positive belief statements (affirmations) to replace them that had words that were of the highest frequencies.

This approach matters because we're not seeking to only remove the dark, clingy beliefs in your life, but also to help you shine your brightest in the world. Throughout your life, you have attracted certain experiences because, at the time they happened, your frequency of vibration as a whole attracted the frequency of that particular experience. What you will now have is a way of looking at each event in your life as an opportunity to heal limiting beliefs and the emotions that accompany them, while removing lower energy viewpoints. Now you have the recipe for doing all of that in this workbook.

Each limiting belief you clear will change not only the frequency of your thoughts, but also the frequency of your very being. Your body will be in a more harmonious state and the experiences you attract will vibrate at higher and higher frequencies, bringing with them the quality of life you really want.

CHAPTER ONE

LIMITING BELIEFS AND THEIR IMPACT

If you always do what you always have done, you will always get what you always got.

—Anonymous

The unhelpful beliefs that we have uncovered for clients vary greatly, from someone unconsciously believing that their muscles are a good place to store unaddressed reactions to life stresses (causing tightness and injuries), to believing that staying overweight will protect them from feeling others' emotions.

Before we uncover limiting beliefs by bringing them into the light, it might help you to consider what belief work is all about. A belief is a thought that your subconscious treats as if it's true and will seek to manifest (in the real world) no matter what. All beliefs are by-products of our surroundings and our social conditioning.

Many beliefs help you make sense of the world and they become a foundation for the actions we take to construct our lives. Limiting beliefs, though, involve restrictive thoughts you weave into the stories you tell yourself about who you and others are, and what your life means.

As the life examples so far illustrate, limiting beliefs can take their toll. They often involve you being held hostage to beliefs you picked up from others. Whose life is it that you are living? Are you willing to keep living as if your purpose was to meet your mother's or father's expectations? Are you trying to live up to the stories you've heard about how a woman or a man should act based on views from others in your inner circle?

Societal beliefs can leave their imprints for decades or longer. For instance, back in the 1940s and 1950s, American women rarely had careers outside the home and were expected to stay home and raise children. Being a housewife is not bad. Expecting every woman to play that role, or women with outside careers to take care of family matters as thoroughly as stay-at-home parents, though, isn't healthy.

Rather than looking to outside factors for your identity, the question becomes, what world would you like to create for yourself? Who is the authentic self behind all the beliefs that have shaped you up until now? Do you like what you see and the lifestyle you have created? If there are some things you'd like to change, we have the tools for creating awareness of your beliefs and designing a more fulfilling, purposeful life.

Limiting beliefs have been discussed by many coaches and authors in the hopes of freeing people from subconscious anchors. This workbook goes a step further by teaching you to directly clear unwanted beliefs. The goal is to help you live the life that you deserve—a life of joy, abundance, and love for yourself and others.

Underlying our approach is the belief that your life is your own responsibility. If you choose to do so, you can learn how to consciously create a healthier reality with your thoughts (which you've been doing unconsciously anyway). All you need is simple awareness of what you've been thinking, and a willingness to trade up limiting thoughts for ones that align better with who you were meant to be. With self-awareness and some emotional elbow grease, you can achieve freedom from the tyranny of unconscious limiting beliefs.

Every belief you hold, whether positive or negative, is entwined with an emotion. Emotions can become a challenge when they linger long enough to have stories that get built around them, that "move in" for the long term. To tell the difference, imagine you have a flash of anger at yourself for, say, trying to multitask and burning your hand on a hot skillet. When the thought "that hurt" is followed by "I'm just stupid!" instead of something like "I need to focus my attention more on what I'm doing," a limiting belief of "I'm stupid" has settled into your mind.

We have found that emotions such as anger that have become trapped in the body often return if the limiting beliefs that reinforce them are not acknowledged and removed. We choose to take the healing process a step further by clearing all the limiting beliefs that surround an unhelpful emotion lodged within you.

How limiting beliefs take shape

Limiting beliefs can become woven into so much of our world. Beliefs are immovable statements made by the mind, solid declarations. For example, "I'm a Democrat," or "I'm a Republican" can be limiting beliefs, as can "If I don't earn a living, I am worthless." These common beliefs can make people highly emotional, causing stronger reactions to situations than may be necessary.

A thought plus a thought, plus a thought becomes a limiting belief. Situations happen, emotions are felt, then thoughts are layered on top in a vain attempt to separate from the pain of the raw emotion. A belief forms from the thoughts that buffer the direct experience of emotion. Emotions then become trapped within the beliefs as unresolved or unfelt. The emotions that become trapped and unresolved within you, potentially leave you numb to knowing you have it, or to feeling other, more enjoyable emotions fully. Meanwhile, the beliefs that cover up that emotion can get stronger as the residue of emotion gets increasingly embedded and gnarly.

Because limiting beliefs affect your emotions, whether you are conscious of them or not, they place limits on your life. In subtle ways, they commonly limit your choices by casting a shadow over your ability to perceive the full range of options available to you in a given circumstance. They affect how you act and react to daily events, undermining choices such as who you love, where you live, the jobs you choose and the risks you take or don't take. These beliefs can also have a major impact on the way you treat everyone from strangers to those closest to you. When triggered by limiting beliefs, any of us can foolishly lash out at our loved ones, leaving a path of destruction in our wake.

In essence, embedded emotions that are energy in the form of emotion are held in place by multiple strands of belief in the form of statements. An embedded emotion is the body's reaction to your mind and the subconscious beliefs held within the mind that were formed as a way to explain outside events. Beliefs that are limiting, or emotions that are limiting, can trap energy in different parts of your mind and body. This trapped energy can feel like it is pulsating inside you, wanting an outlet to free itself. A situation comes along, say, a car unexpectedly cuts you off in traffic and you think, "how rude" (or maybe even, "you @#*&!") Your stomach churns from the incident. Later in the day it happens again! Some other jerk cuts you off in traffic. Those strong emotions could plant a seed that turns your thoughts into the full-fledged belief of, "I always get cut off by jerks in traffic!"

Whether the belief triggered by your emotional response to something is positive or negative, it affects you, oftentimes repeatedly. Besides narrowing your reality, the repeated triggering in your body of a stuck limiting belief can also greatly stress your bodily systems – specifically, your adrenal glands. A limiting belief will weigh you down by lowering the frequency and vibrance of your life force and affecting the way you function in your day-to-day life.

As you eradicate limiting beliefs with this workbook, you will find that you still experience difficult times, but will look at these events very differently. The difference will be noticeable when old beliefs are no longer triggered, or you recognize them as just being stories. When you reach that point, you will be able to see things from a perspective of gratitude because you will have learned to connect with and trust the grounded part of yourself that is separate from specific circumstances. That gratitude will naturally change your reactions to any event. When you know your unhelpful beliefs well enough to deactivate them, you'll find that you simply lead a healthier and less stressful life.

The storylines of limiting beliefs – how you let them have their way.

Suppose for a moment that there is a job opening where you work. It's a dream job and you have always wanted a chance at it. The new title would make you feel proud, the tasks would be exciting and challenging, not to mention the pay increase you would receive. However, instead of jumping on the opportunity you say to yourself, "I will wait a day or two to decide about applying."

After a few days, you have still not taken any steps towards getting the new job. You make excuses and say to yourself, "Well, I never went to school for that and I am sure I would be up against more qualified people, maybe it is just best that I just stay where I am and I can try for a different position the next time."

Just like that, you have allowed the opportunity to pass. Someone else gets the job and it hurts. Yet you come up with a dozen reasons for why you didn't want the job after all. Did you ever stop to consider there might be a limiting belief creating that hesitation? Oh, and by the way, this was the third perfectly good job opening you passed up this year.

Perhaps there is a love interest that you would really like to get to know better. He or she isn't wearing a ring and talks to you at lunch, yet you feel there is an invisible wall that won't allow you to fully connect or reach out. When you do talk, you never seek more from the interactions because of concern you aren't attractive enough, or don't feel worthy of someone great. Self-defeating chatter echoes in your mind as you tell yourself that the situation would be too complicated or he/she might reject you. Later, that person ends up dating a colleague and you sigh over the chance you missed out on.

If you take a moment to process the thinking behind situations you've experienced like these, you might uncover entire lists of limiting beliefs that prevented you from acting on opportunities. In some cases, the beliefs might even be unconscious ones (which the tools in chapter three can help you uncover).

Here are some beliefs that may have led to the above missed opportunities.

Limiting beliefs about applying for a new job:

> *I don't have the qualities it takes to be successful.*
> *I am not talented enough.*
> *I fear competition.*
> *I am not good enough.*
> *I'm not educated enough.*
> *My skills are not valued by society.*

Some less noticeable beliefs might be:

> *I don't deserve an abundant life.*
> *God doesn't want me to have a good life.*
> *I must suffer in order to be successful.*
> *I'm not worthy of being taken seriously.*
> *I'm afraid to fail at meeting others' expectations.*
> *I haven't done enough to deserve true success.*
> *I haven't proven myself enough to deserve true success.*

With the love interest example, potential limiting beliefs are:

> *I'm unworthy of a loving relationship.*
> *Nobody wants somebody like me.*
> *I am terrified of rejection.*
> *Relationships are too complicated to fit into my life.*
> *I am not attractive enough.*

Relationships are too much hard work.
Relationships are painful.

Limiting beliefs affect you on many levels because beliefs are energy. We have beliefs about everything from politics, religion, relationships, ourselves, money, health and love—all the way to the very mundane. We can have strong beliefs about the cars we drive, brand name shoes, vacation options, even which side of the bed we sleep on!

You might be thinking, if everyone suffers from limiting beliefs, why do the work of clearing them? Without them, what would happen?

The reasons to clear limiting beliefs are numerous: improved health, peace of mind, and opening up your life to endless possibilities as you gain greater emotional and behavioral flexibility. Eventually you will experience life without judgment and feel more love on a daily basis.

By eliminating unhelpful beliefs, you remove limits on your ability to create improvement in any area of life. Clearing beliefs changes the way you react to situations that come up in your life. Instead of reacting irrationally and with judgment, you can remain neutral, even while recognizing that a situation is upsetting on some levels.

The bottom line: If you do clearing work, a greater sense of peace, among other things, will be your reward. Others around you will notice how grounded you are, and may become curious about your change. Perhaps their interest will provide opportunities to share this work.

Beliefs from the outside world

We pick up all kinds of beliefs throughout life based on our experiences and seeing people in action. To understand core beliefs, it helps to see how they differ and overlap with the other types. The three major types of beliefs are inherited beliefs, core beliefs and societal beliefs:

Inherited beliefs often come from your mother and father, and can affect aspects of your vitality such as your health. These beliefs often cause you to look for proof to reinforce what you believe is reality because of trusting your elders, whose views the belief likely helped support. Perhaps you hold a belief of, "I have stomach aches and digestive issues because my mother had them." You had witnessed as a child your mother's stomach troubles; as a result, with the ongoing digestive challenges you developed as an adult, you assume you simply inherited the health condition. In fact, we suspect that a majority of health difficulties are likely the result of beliefs about the inevitability of them developing, rather than the result of already having physical factors that may inevitably cause a particular disease.

This book focuses on core beliefs that were created from your personal experiences during childhood and are the very essence of how you view yourself and others. Our core beliefs, unbeknownst to us at times, work to shape our future. In addition to having your worldview shaped by family and/or early caregivers (inherited beliefs), childhood is when you encountered various people and situations in which you took on the beliefs of those in authority. In this way, you began to form fundamental beliefs about the outside world, your place in it and even how you should react to it. Core beliefs often are not challenged until later in life when a person's perception changes from a teenager to that of an adult.

Societal beliefs are beliefs based upon cultural expectations of how to behave. These beliefs not only affect your worldview, but the opportunities your community may offer you. Religious beliefs and generational beliefs like the housewife example discussed earlier stem from the society we feel connected to and shape our behaviors and who we allow ourselves to become. Religions involve a belief in one or more divine beings, along with a set of practices and a moral code that help to reinforce shared beliefs and faith in a divine source.

These societal beliefs leak in from unexpected places such as radio talk shows, TV commercials, other kids on the playground, books, magazines, Hollywood icons, religious leaders and politicians.

How we spread limiting beliefs

Face it, limiting beliefs have monumental effects on us all. It may be difficult to hear to be sure, but just as your beliefs can help you create an amazing life, they can help you create your own pain and add to the suffering of others. Maybe you already have lost a relationship or two, or have disconnected from family with whom you were once close due to vastly different belief systems. Maybe you have built layers of beliefs surrounding unforgiveness and love that have increased the distance between you and family members. Limiting beliefs can create walls around us that keep those we love on the outside.

As an example, consider a young father, stern in nature and strong in work ethic. He might be the type of man to have adopted an inherited belief that "the opinion of others is most important in life," and another belief of, "I must be critical of others in order to feel safe." We can probably assume that his children will grow up hyper-vigilant of their surroundings and of other's opinions. His children would thus carry on the burden of living life in a state of low-grade anxiety from having to walk on eggshells around everyone, while thinking that they have to be critical of others and expecting the same treatment from them. No wonder some children cannot wait to move out of the house at 18!

The catch is, these inherited beliefs follow us well into adulthood. For example, a woman who lived through the Great Depression and struggled to survive could develop a core belief of, "I must struggle in order to make ends meet." Eventually her children may adopt the same beliefs, and feel like "life is a constant upward struggle," or "it is necessary to struggle in order to live," and "I must suffer in order to live."

The belief that "suffering is life" is a burden that was amplified by the harsh reality of the environment the mother experienced, imprinting many layers of beliefs for this lady and shaping her world and that of her children. With the application of simple energetic tools, she could have banished many of these limiting beliefs from her mind in a matter of minutes. She wouldn't have been held back by the perceived limitations of her environment if they hadn't been fostered by her mind. She would have become free from the subconscious restrictions that she grew up with. Her children would have grown up free from them as well.

By clearing major beliefs surrounding past family dynamics, you can easily dissolve related internal friction and conflict. When you work on replacing all limiting beliefs formed in childhood, your past resentments can fade, and your current relationships can then be built on forgiveness, trust and love.

Journaling to solidify what you have learned:

Now that you understand what limiting beliefs are, think about how those beliefs have shaped your thoughts, and ultimately your life, up to this point. Record what you notice.

_____

_____

_____

_____

_____

_____

_____

CHAPTER TWO

THE "HOW TO" OF CLEARING BELIEFS

"Mastering others makes you strong; mastering yourself makes you fearless."

—Unknown

Our work with many clients has given us front-row seats to life-transforming experiences. The fact that you're reading this book means you are ready for some life altering of your own. Understand that you will still be yourself, just upgraded. Get ready for you — Version 2.0!

Before this enhanced new self can be fully integrated, there will be a time of shifting whenever you let go of outdated limiting beliefs. A released limiting belief can hold a tremendous amount of energy, especially if it stems from an emotionally charged event. The emotions surrounding beliefs can be stored in any body system, which can lead to chronic stress of those body systems.

When you clear a belief, underneath that, energetically speaking, emotions lurk. You may experience heavy feelings and you may not feel like yourself for a few days. Understand your body's limitations and be gentle with clearing beliefs. You may have to take periodic breaks to integrate the new affirmations you incorporate into your body while processing outdated beliefs.

We have learned through the process of belief work that we have done (for ourselves and with clients) that it is possible to experience that processing in the form of physical or emotional symptoms while the body, mind and spirit become restored. Physical symptoms of this healing process, such as random aches and pains, dizziness and nausea are just an indication that a good thing is happening. Give your body time to recover, as it usually does not take longer than a few days to a week for your body to work through fully processing energetic upgrades you have made.

Some cleared beliefs will affect you very little. However, there will be times when clearing a particular belief will bring on the waterworks! Don't worry, you're not broken, you are just releasing and healing. Any releasing symptoms (from sighing, coughing, sneezing, chills, to feeling exhausted, and of course crying or sobbing) are perfectly normal. Your body will respond in a way that is unique to you. Tell yourself, "I give myself permission to take all the time I need and to feel all I need to feel in order to heal all limiting beliefs." Sit with your discomfort, as a new way of living is being created.

Once the processing ends, you may suddenly find there is so much space and functionality that wasn't there before. The relief you feel can be highly exhilarating and, best of all, you will be able to breathe more deeply.

Don't try to hasten the work, or feel pressured to clear hundreds of beliefs all at once. The healing that comes from clearing beliefs is a process of uncovering each individual layer that wasn't serving you, and for you becoming a more conscious individual. This is your journey, and you get to set the pace.

The Physical Imprint of Limiting Beliefs

The medical world is finally catching on to the understanding that buried beliefs have a tremendous impact on our physical health even more than lifestyle choices such as food and diet.

Our beliefs rule our biology. Bruce Lipton, Ph.D., in his book The Biology of Belief (2005), explains, "Our mind has dominion over our physical state by establishing our beliefs as well as our perceptions about the state of our overall health." For instance, you've likely heard about the placebo effect. In well-designed studies, it has been found that when subjects didn't know if they were getting a real medicine or a sugar pill, those receiving sugar pills still dramatically improved! When people believe that a medicine has a high cure rate and they take it, they often begin to feel better immediately.

The consequence of the powerful grip that the mind can have over the body is that, if someone believes that a disease like diabetes is a death sentence and that person gets diabetes, he or she might become more sickly just from adopting that particular societal belief. Another example is the statement, "You have six to eight months to live." If you choose to believe that statement, you may in fact have exactly that much time to live. Likewise, deeply believing that you can manifest full healing related to a health condition by shifting your unconscious beliefs can greatly increase your chances of overcoming it.

Note that we're not advocating that you ignore something like a cancer diagnosis or diabetes. There may be a very real reason that you are going through the experience of having and being treated for an illness as part of your journey on Earth. The importance of seeking advice from licensed medical professionals about your health doesn't negate the value that your beliefs have in the healing process, or the safety of belief clearing work as you undergo medical treatment.

At the heart of symptoms

Take heart disease for instance, which remains the leading cause of death in the United States. The costs for treating heart conditions are enormous, and recovery often includes improving diet and lifestyle; but are those really the origin of these diseases? Lipton notes, "People don't necessarily inherit a greater genetic risk for a disease; they instead inherit the belief in the inevitability of developing the disease."

Working as a kinesiologist, Mayline has seen proof every day that emotions directly affect health. In the popular book You Can Heal Your Life (1984), Louise Hay says that, "Illness, however mild or severe, is an indicator of your emotional state, caused by your thoughts and focus." Hay goes on to describe how a physical symptom can be created by repeating a mental habit. We now know that an unhelpful repetitive mental habit is something that does not benefit the body. Repeatedly exposing the body to this mental habit over time, Hay noted, can eventually create an illness. For instance, repeatedly reliving a past trauma of grief over the death of a loved one can place an emotional burden on the body that impacts the quality of lung function. Should those emotions linger in the lung area, you could develop a susceptibility to bronchitis or pneumonia.

By using an affirmation to replace a limiting mental habit, you could heal an illness and/or organ or gland. For instance, in working as a kinesiologist, Mayline has found that many clients with heart issues or lingering pain in their left shoulder and neck area report significant improvement within a few short visits after clearing limiting beliefs in the energy center associated with the heart about self-love, self-forgiveness, and forgiveness of others. These clients' physical symptoms appeared to result from harmful beliefs that blocked the ability of love to come into what is called a heart chakra. While many healers focus on helping people by clearing their body of individual emotions, we like to take Hay's ideas a step further. We have come to realize through years of practice that an unhelpful emotion held in the body is actually tied to a belief statement that puts limits on every area of your life, including your body and its ability to heal. Clearing limiting belief statements must be addressed for anyone to go into deeper healing when it comes to a health challenge.

Your subconscious self-talk may go something like this: "Because my grandmother had heart disease, then it's likely I'll get it too." Regardless of whether you accept this or not, it is our personal opinion that anybody can change their life and the quality of their health through the act of clearing outdated beliefs related to personal ideas and identities concerning health. We will discuss limiting beliefs on specific health topics in a future workbook, as long-standing health issues can have many layers of beliefs needing to be individually addressed.

How the body retains certain beliefs

From years of assisting clients, we have seen how particular beliefs affect not only someone's emotional state but certain body systems. In particular, the human body has an energetic field. As noted by Barbara Brennan and others, this human energy field is part of the universal field of energy that connects all things. The human energy field consists of layers of energy that extend out from the skin and cover all its surfaces as if they were larger layers of skin. The deepest energy layer is often called the emotional body, and is the layer of energy surrounding the body one to three inches above your skin. Sometimes called the etheric body, this emotional body is also considered the first, lowest layer of your aura which is a part of our body that we don't see but oftentimes sense instead. It is noted to be in immediate contact with your physical body.

Because of its close connection to the physical body, sometimes when we feel emotional, we will attribute a pain to the physical body when it is actually this etheric layer that is jarred or wounded. For instance, this can happen when you hold on to absorbed energy from a big fight with a boyfriend or girlfriend. You can feel the emotions still lingering in your stomach or neck from the heated conversation and need downtime to process it physically. Emotions or traumas from your past can also affect you in the etheric, or emotional body. Its makeup is unique to each individual as it contains all the person's current feelings and those that they've held onto from unresolved issues in the past.

The emotional or etheric layer is connected to areas of energy (chakras) that connect to certain locations in the physical body. The word "chakra" translates as wheel or disk, and in a sense these are wheels or disks of energy. Imagine swirling energy wheels where matter and consciousness meet. These wheels of vital life force energy keep us alive, vibrant and healthy. Although this energy is invisible to the naked eye, some healers and gifted empaths can visualize or sense these chakras with amazing clarity using their intuitive, inner sight. With practice, anyone can learn to see and feel chakras!

By releasing limiting core beliefs that are obstructing the flow of energy in chakras associated with certain areas of the body, you can make the energy field of those chakras lighter.

How you know if you have beliefs to clear?

Anybody with a pulse has limiting beliefs, including you. Ultimately it has been your beliefs that have shaped and defined your life, though you might not understand how. It is also likely that you are in the dark about some limiting beliefs hidden from your conscious mind. Heightened emotional responses to people or events are the clue. Think about a person you easily become frustrated with or can't stand. Whoever you just pictured is a huge, flashing, neon sign that says, *trigger*! What is it about that person that gets under your skin? Stopping to explore the emotions you experience will reveal a treasure trove of misdirected energy stored in your unconscious.

Your daily routine can also offer numerous clues to your personal triggers. You sleep through your alarm clock again! Why? Could it be because you don't feel fulfillment in your job? There is a trigger. Your kids argue on the way to school and you feel like you are losing your mind. There is another trigger. If you suddenly find yourself out of control, sad, irritated or simply emotionally shut down, those are indications that you need to pay attention to the messages your body is sending you through your emotions and actions.

When you react to events with emotions such as defensiveness, anger and frustration, apathy or depression- those emotions are keys to unlocking those parts of yourself that require healing. As hard as it is to accept, you feel the most resentment and anger with people or situations that mirror your own shortcomings. That's because your responses to life will always reflect your own issues. You might think getting rid of the person or situation in your life that triggers you will make you happy. What will really happen is that another person or situation with the same irritating tendencies will show up to deliver the very same challenges you need to work through. All of this happens because the limiting beliefs you need to become conscious of still require your awareness and some clearing work.

Journaling to solidify what you have learned:

The above paragraphs were examples of how to be aware of feelings triggered in your daily life by recognizing emotional responses and patterns that you have to people and situations. Now that you have a better idea of what triggering feels like, journal some thoughts concerning the areas in which you tend to feel triggered. Later as you work through the beliefs in this book, circle back and see what beliefs came up as needing clearing related to areas below that you suspected held triggers for you.

_____

_____

_____

_____

_____

_____

CHAPTER THREE

METHODS TO THE MADNESS: OVERCOMING LIMITING BELIEFS

"It is through the simplicity of our thoughts that the world can be filled with magic or misery."

—*Unknown*

We have been studying limiting beliefs for years and have found that the biggest challenge people experience is figuring out their own limiting beliefs. Remember, these beliefs are usually subconscious. Until you develop a habit of addressing limiting beliefs, uncovering particular ones can be difficult except when a situation triggers a reaction. A trigger is an event that instigates strong emotions within you that you may not know you have. These strong emotions can be linked to past emotional trauma or painful experiences that you were attached to and did not fully process at the time, eventually becoming a belief.

Your belief-clearing team

How then can you become aware of hidden beliefs that are not from an obvious trigger? Your subconscious holds the key. What you are reading contains a road map to the potential blocks of a more vibrant life that are hiding in your subconscious. What this workbook will give you is a number of energetic tools to use to dig them out. We've done much of the work for you by compiling a collection of limiting beliefs that you can work with right away. First, let's define the factors that you will be working with as you clear beliefs throughout this workbook.

The subconscious mind

The subconscious is where all information associated with experiences are recorded and stored, as well as storing knowledge (facts and ideas) and wisdom (discernment about how to approach situations). The subconscious contains memories from all experiences in which you had a reaction. The subconscious mind may have kicked in if you are feeling your defensive mechanisms activate, or feel fear, isolation or an urge to survive a situation.

You can think of the subconscious as a reservoir for emotions outside of the conscious mind; as a subliminal place, or place of partial perceptions; as your innermost self, your inner psyche or your imagination; and as the place where past memories, including dormant, repressed or suppressed memories, are stored.

Every subconscious memory is an incomplete experience that our soul has not fully understood. Collectively, these memories can be called your "shadow side" because the subconscious houses negative emotions attached to charged stories and memories in the form of buried beliefs.

All this information is programmed into the cellular memory of the physical body and our DNA. Wisdom is gained as you see how your responses to life experiences play out. This assimilation process works well when the beliefs that become a part of yourself improve your positive connections with the world. But it's more common to develop beliefs that limit your options and don't truly protect you.

The subconscious is so insanely powerful that it won't let go of a belief until you deliberately tell it to let go—and to replace it with a new, better command. Yes, surprisingly, the subconscious can be programmed to work the way you want it to, much like training a computer or a robot. Help comes in the form of events that serve as triggers to literally rattle out an old hurt that has lodged in your subconscious, while awakening related, outdated convictions and perceptions of what the experience meant.

Deliberately reprogramming your subconscious through belief work gives you the conscious power to change everything you currently feel ill-at-ease about.

The conscious mind

The conscious mind is a thinker and observer of the world through the five senses. It has free will, and provides your worldly identity, answering the question, "Who am I?" It focuses on current awareness only and an immediate responses to that awareness; the conscious mind has a moving, in-the-moment, attachment to the meaning of things, and connects to short-term memory (Detzler).

Suppose there was a wrestling match between your conscious mind and your subconscious mind; the subconscious would always win. Even if your conscious mind is convinced wholeheartedly of your belief in something, that won't matter if the subconscious part of your mind holds hidden beliefs that counter this "firmly held" conviction. Because of what may be an unknown subconscious block, you cannot seem to gain ground against whatever situation involves the trigger and hidden belief. Therefore, you may struggle daily with the same issues, feeling as if you're going no place.

Regardless of your faith or religious background (and whether you believe in a higher power or not), you can notice a trigger or heightened emotional response to something and use that response as a prompt for the conscious mind to come to the rescue. This involves harnessing your analytical mind to pull out the old subconscious programming and replace it with new commands. But first, your conscious mind has to use its powers of awareness to focus on what it is up against, and marshal forces beyond those you may typically draw on.

Keywords for understanding the conscious mind:

Self identity
Personal self
No memory or short term memory
"Who am I?"
Moving attachment of meaning
Free will
Current awareness
Awake
Aware and responding to one's awareness

God and your Higher Self (The Superconscious Mind)

Who is God and what is your Higher Self? Although you don't have to share this belief to do clearing work, we believe our bodies would be nothing without the essence of a positive energy that many refer to as God. God is the source of all of life, of all energy, and is all around us in every living thing, having many names. You are a spark of that divine energy. Your Higher Self refers to that spark, the part of you that is God.

When you connect with God and/or your Higher Self, you energetically rise above your thoughts and ego state of mind. Have you ever had an almost surreal experience where you left your normal thinking state of mind and were aligned to a broader state of being where you became fully aware of the higher truth of a situation? That is an example of experiencing a shift into your Higher Self, in which you free yourself from your ego state of self.

Ego refers to the part of us that is a false form of self-identification. Some refer to ego as that which is "edging God out." By rising above your ego self, whether through meditation, setting intentions or saying affirmations, you can more easily access that higher part of yourself, your Superconscious Mind. It is this Higher Self within you that co-creates the world you occupy, through Higher Self interactions with your conscious mind.

Your Higher Self also is the part of you that is connected to others and to all of consciousness, which together become the flow of life. We will explain how to connect with this universal energy of Higher Self later in this workbook.

We want to be clear that no matter your faith or spiritual background you are a spiritual being in our eyes, first and foremost. Whatever concept you choose to use to acknowledge the Divine is perfectly acceptable, and you can substitute that concept in places where we have used God/Higher Self in upcoming text.

Some keywords that are used to describe Higher Self, aka your Superconscious Mind, are:

Unconditional love
All loving thoughts

Trust
Intuition
Unconditional forgiveness
Understanding
Freedom
God
Divine Source
Interconnectedness
Joy
Direct knowing
Transcending normal consciousness

The simplicity of clearing beliefs

Even knowing that you have team members on your side, you may still harbor concerns about do-it-yourself healing work and whether you can handle it. If something appears complex, studies show that people often give it more value. However, clearing beliefs is truly one of the simplest, yet most powerful, things you can do for self-care. With a little trust in yourself, you are capable of connecting easily to life-enhancing guidance at any time. Sometimes you may feel triggered by an emotional exchange with a loved one and a limiting belief such as, "I feel out of control when my partner doesn't agree 100 percent with me." With one of the methods we will explain in this book, you can clear that belief and its associated feeling of overwhelm in less than 30 seconds. With added practice, you will soon have a healthy tool for squelching any thoughts that become out of hand.

People from any walk of life can succeed at clearing beliefs using the approaches in this workbook. Clearing limiting beliefs will change how you look at your world. The more you clear, the more you will advance in your consciousness. What we mean is that the more you clear and become aware of in your subconscious the more you become consciously aware, and that is how we all release ignorance and achieve freedom from suffering.

Start with what you are complaining about. Your complaints are showing you what triggers you. Is it a family member, some recent news, or something at work? Sometimes beliefs to clear show up as repeated frustrations in your life such as, "Every time I leave for vacation, something bad happens." And crazily enough, when you believe that, challenging things do come up right before you leave on vacation. The more you dig into a specific situation, the more layers of beliefs you may find need to be cleared so you can feel more peace when encountering those situations again. Often times it can be good to ask a friend what it is that you complain about the most. What they say may surprise you, yet that would be a good place to start.

The key to clearing beliefs is to have a pure intention to do just that, and to stay relaxed to allow your conscious mind and subconscious to work together. By the simple act of intention, you will instruct the subconscious to clear a belief that doesn't sit right with you. This comes after establishing an energetic connection with your Higher Self.

Clearing Methods

To clear your limiting beliefs, we have compiled five methods that we simplified after working with many clients. Whether you are a visually oriented person, logic-driven, spiritual or feeling oriented, one of these methods will suit you. You can simply choose which one resonates the best to use on yourself. You can also do this work as an adjunct when seeing other energy healers, chiropractors or any number of health practitioners.

Ultimately, you are the master of your experiences and you know the nuances of your body, mind and health better than anyone. Therefore you know the areas you need to work on the most. No one can step into the light and change your life except you.

Here are the tools we recommend you consider to do that:

Visually Washing Beliefs Away

Imagine standing on a beach with your back to the waves. You are holding a long piece of driftwood in your hands. The wood has been smoothed by the friction of the sand and waves. It is bleached by the sun and is old and dry, weighing very little for its size. Now use that driftwood to write one of your limiting beliefs in the sand before you. You can write it as big or as small as you want. If the belief runs deep, maybe you'll want to dig the driftwood in deeper into the sand as you write it. Observe what you have written and feel the cold waves wash around your ankles and back out to the ocean. Again the waves wash in, chilling your legs, covering the belief that you have written. As the waves recede, make it your intention to allow all connections and any emotional or other residue attached to that belief to be completely washed away by the ocean waves. For particularly "sticky" beliefs it might help to watch the waves move in and cover your outdated belief several times. You will know when it has finally left. You might either feel it release in the area of your solar plexus chakra or you might no longer see a trace of it in your visualization, followed by a knowing that you are free from it. Trust yourself.

Visual Obliteration Method

For you action movie fans, visualize a belief written on a TV like screen and then blow it to smithereens! Along the same lines, you can light the statement on fire and watch it burn away. Burning can be done literally by writing beliefs down on a piece of paper, or as a visualization where you write them down and place them into an imaginary fire. Either way, as the beliefs burn away, feel them leave your space. If you don't have a safe way of having a fire, but want the same feeling of satisfaction instead use a common office shredder. This will work wonders for belief clearing too.

Visual Erasing Method

For the academics among you, it might be more comfortable to visualize your limiting belief written on a chalkboard or whiteboard. When you're ready to let go of it, erase the belief with an eraser. Simple as that. It is the intention that is important. As long as you see it gone, know that it is.

Prayer Method

For some it might feel right to clear a belief with prayer. Here is one that is simple to use and works quickly. It works as follows:

Write out limiting beliefs you want to clear on a piece of paper. Include all the beliefs you know are limiting to you. You will know because reading them or saying them might make you feel triggered in some way, including a twinge felt in your gut or just feeling unsettled as you read them. Write as many as you recognize on a piece of paper, then place your hand on the whole list of limiting beliefs and say, "Thank you God for clearing this particular belief (or these multiple beliefs) from every part of my being. Thank you for healing the wounds and for the lessons that were created by having this/these beliefs, and thank you now for replacing them with the truth. Amen." Shred or throw away the paper of old beliefs. Or if you are so inclined, keep the list as a touchstone to celebrate your growth later.

Manual Clearing Method

Another method that is more of a left brain approach uses a technique or cue word along with the help of your Higher Self, which will instruct the mind and the subconscious to clear the belief. This method can appeal to those who are the more logical, intellectual types, and who might not be drawn to meditation or visualization. Here are steps to "manually" or intentionally "pull" the beliefs using a hand motion. The hand motion is simply grabbing an envisioned belief as if it were a loose thread to be pulled from your heart and chest area, pulling it away from you until you feel a release. Once pulled out simply throw the belief away. Use a command phrase such as, "Pull, dissolve, and cancel" while physically pulling a limiting belief that you are intending to clear. God and your Higher Self will act together to go into your subconscious mind and literally pull, dissolve and cancel that particular limiting belief based on your intention to do so.

The belief may be a long-held one from your early perceptions of life, an inherited belief, or a societal belief that you unwittingly accepted. It can be a belief surrounding whatever area of life you are experiencing some difficulty in, such as moving to a new location or changing jobs. For instance, you may create a roadblock to a more fulfilling experience by beliefs that include, "Moving always takes longer than it should" or "Change equals loss." To begin this approach, settle your energy by grounding yourself through a meditation to be fully present with yourself. Then, connect to your higher self by simply asking to connect. You can use your own form of invocation or something as simple as, "God and I are connected and we work together as one."

Now that you are connected to your Higher Self, with the help of God, your subconscious mind is ready to be instructed to have a particular belief pulled from every compartment of your subconscious and it will be so.

Keep in mind that this method is flexible. You can use whatever command phrase feels right as an alternative to, "Pull, dissolve, cancel."

Other command options include:

I command my subconscious mind to clear all beliefs of...
Transmute and dissolve all negative aspects of...
Erase, dissolve and cancel...
Cancel, pull and erase all...
Release, dissolve and transmute...
Erase and eliminate...

Or you can use:

God dissolve my belief that limits me.
God, please clear all unwanted beliefs and replace with good.
Source of all life, please erase, eliminate and replace with good.

The Importance of Tapping

The clearing process can leave an empty energetic space or void that must be filled. Tapping allows your body to get present with itself and allows you to direct your subconscious mind to create a new, positively held belief. The added step of tapping in a life-affirming beliefs leaves you feeling more balanced after your personal session. When you tap in affirmations, which are the positive aspect of the specific limiting belief being tackled, the process rewires your brain. Over time as you clear beliefs, it will start to transform your outer life. For the scenarios above, someone might use the affirmation, "Moving always happens with ease," or "Change equals growth."

The act of tapping helps to bypass your conscious mind so that you connect directly with your subconscious, reprogramming the new belief. It's about upgrading the wiring for your brain.

Sharing Belief-Clearing Work

Belief work is such a powerful tool and the more you use it, the more you will appreciate its impact on your experience of life. You may feel compelled to share this work with others as a result. That is a wonderful gift to give. Yet you may find many are not ready. Many people have held beliefs for a long time, and even if a belief is unpleasant or judgmental in nature, it is familiar. It can be hard for anyone to let go of the past. If you have ever known someone fighting an addiction, you might have learned that the person has to be ready to get help; by forcing them to face their addiction before they are open and willing to do so, you will likely push them away. Belief work is no different.

Allow your friends and family to be where they are—lead by example and just share how clearing work has improved your experiences. Clean up the limiting beliefs you have personally about the person or situation, and let them have the time they need to move forward at their own pace. Trust that the people in your life who are not ready for changing their belief systems will come to a point on their own when they are ready. Just be patient and work on you.

Preparing yourself for belief clearing

Before you dive into clearing limiting beliefs, tackling a few preparatory statements early on will allow deeper healing. Doing his preparatory work early in your clearing practice will help to shift you into a higher state of consciousness. Consider using whichever clearing methods that you feel most comfortable with.

Address the following limiting beliefs about doing clearing work:

> *Healing therapies never work for me.*
> *I have tried many things to change my life with no results.*
> *Limiting beliefs don't really make that much difference.*
> *If I try new therapies, I will fail.*
> *Clearing beliefs is acting like God.*
> *Clearing beliefs will be too painful for me.*
> *Even if clearing beliefs works, it won't keep working.*
> *Results from healing therapies are not lasting.*
> *Results from healing therapies are not instant.*
> *Limiting beliefs come back, even if I clear them.*
> *It's normal that healing modalities never work for me.*
> *My limiting beliefs are too powerful to be overcome.*

Positive affirmations to tap in about clearing limiting beliefs:

> *My results from clearing beliefs are permanent and lasting.*
> *I am open and willing to experiencing new healing therapies.*
> *Clearing beliefs are easy and effortless for me to clear on my own.*
> *Once a limiting belief is cleared, I know it is clear.*
> *It's normal for me that all healing modalities work for me in some way.*
> *Overcoming my limiting beliefs are easy and effortless.*

In addition, we've found that someone cannot clear limiting beliefs unless she or he makes a personal connection with the source of their vitality, perhaps God/Higher Self.

Part of the beauty of life is that everyone's personal connection is unique. Ultimately, anything that helps you to feel more connected to the world around you can be considered a spiritual touchstone. You may feel more connected and energetic when you are out in nature, or while gardening or running outdoors. Or that spiritual connection may be tied to a place that you consider sacred, such as a temple or a church. Regardless, we believe that nothing is more important than a person's personal connection to source.

See the end of this chapter to learn more about fully connecting with your life source. In the meantime, you can clear limiting beliefs for yourself to enhance your God/Higher Self/life force connection.

To assist deep subconscious and inner-child healing, try some of these prep-work affirmations to dissolve barriers to full healing:

My inner child releases all fear of answering the questions.
My inner child releases all resistance to the answers.
I give my subconscious mind permission to answer the questions.
My subconscious releases all forms of lying/defensiveness in order to protect itself.
My inner child releases all forms of denial in order to protect itself.
My subconscious releases all forms of self-denial in order to protect itself.
My mental body releases all forms of resistance in order to protect itself from answering the questions.
My emotional body releases all forms of resistance.
My ego releases all forms of defensiveness in order to protect itself.
I am healed instantly and on all layers and in all dimensions.
My body is self-healing and self-regenerating.

Affirmations you can tap in to encourage deeper healing include:

I can be healed instantly.
My inner child is aware of her/his complete healing and wholeness.
I am in harmony with my inner child.
I can allow myself to be healed instantly.
Good health is my birthright.
I am connected to God/Spirit/Higher power) at all times.
My body is self-healing; my body is self-regenerating.
I know what it feels like to be healed instantly.
I know how to be in harmony with God/Higher Self.
I know what it feels like to rise above my thoughts and tune into spirit.
I know how to live free from identifying with my mind.
I know how to live free from identifying through my ego.

Address the following beliefs that may be obstructing a clear connection to God/Higher Self:

I am fearful of being judged for believing my unique beliefs.
I feel guilty/doubtful concerning the unique beliefs I have about God.
I am limited in my ability to connect with God/Higher self.
There is a barrier that I must push through in order to connect with God/Higher Self.
I feel doubtful of God's ability to heal me fully.
I must strive to connect to God/Higher Self.
I'm terrified of being abandoned by God/Higher Self.
I am limited in my ability to heal myself through God.
Without being connected to God/ Higher Self am ineffective.
I doubt that God is within me any time I need.
I am uncertain I am fully connected to God/ Higher Self .

My ego gets in the way of feeling fully connected to God/Higher Self.

I can never trust God or myself completely.

Affirmations to replace old limiting beliefs that are restricting your connection to God/Higher Self include:

I know how to be fully connected to God/Higher Self with complete certainty.

It is normal for me to always feel connected to God/Higher Self.

By being an instrument of love, I fulfill my destiny and purpose.

It is normal for me to feel full of love for others and myself.

My heart is never separate from God.

Being connected to God, I fulfill my destiny and purpose.

I know how to live my day-to-day life free from ego

I know how to live in harmony with my ego.

I know how to be in harmony with my spiritual self.

I allow myself to be capable of consistent, unconditional love for others, and my heart is never weary.

I let go of all attachment regarding the material things of life in order to be an instrument of Love.

I can have a healthy ego while maintaining a relationship with my Higher Self/God.

I release all fears of failure that I cannot connect fully to God.

I know what it feels like to never again feel separated from my Higher Self/God.

I feel worthy of God's guidance and love.

I am never separated from God's guidance or love.

I am never separated from the guidance of my Higher Self.

I am secure in God's guidance.

I am secure in the guidance of my Higher Self.

I accept the highest expression of my intuition.

I accept that I am a part of God and can therefore never be separate.

I can be strong in the stillness of my own mind yet open to my Higher Self/God.

It is normal for me to feel connected to my Higher Self/God at all times.

Some added clearing tools to use in your belief clearing work

Muscle testing yourself

Muscle testing is a simple way for anyone to access their Higher Self, or, in other words, their higher intuitive power or inner intuition. This powerful technique has been around since the 1930's when chiropractor George Goodheart started using it in his practice. He did so to uncover energy blockages that were not necessarily related to structural challenges in the skeleton, but to muscle and energetic imbalances in the body. He found that the response of muscles to a statement could be used as a surrogate that provides information about the body's energetic imbalances. Since then, muscle testing has become an alternative healing tool that can tap into the emotional, mental/psychological and and spiritual blocks in someone's life, as addressed by a number of healing modalities.

Muscle testing is a natural, non-invasive diagnostic tool that allows you or someone else to ask your body "yes" or "no" questions regarding a myriad things. It works with the idea that a positive association strengthens a muscle that is being used as a barometer of what is going on in the body. On the other hand, a negative thought, substance or traumatic experience will weaken a muscle used for testing (indicator muscle). For instance, many people will have an indicator muscle go weak if they think of a word that has bad connotations for them, such as "no" or "anger" or "loneliness." Bypassing the conscious mind, the muscle test can go straight to the subconscious and intuitive energy systems of the body, when done in combination with the tester accessing their Higher Self. We recommend the book Touch for Health: The Complete Edition (2005) by John and Matthew Thie to further understand muscle testing. With a little faith and practice, you can learn muscle testing and have it be a healing tool that helps your personal journey.

Bradley Nelson, another chiropractor, in his book The Emotion Code (2007) reveals how people can use self-testing methods to release trapped and toxic emotions that have settled within their bodies from past traumas and upsets. We reference Nelson's book because of its simple description of self- testing methods that anyone can practice. Below are a few favorite self-testing techniques for you to experiment with to see which one or two works well for you to use to find limiting beliefs for the remainder of this book. As a reminder, we believe in the healing of clearing trapped emotions. But you can take your healing a step further by clearing limiting beliefs that are being triggered at the same time as you are having a strong emotional reaction. The belief associated with the emotion ultimately is what has caused the trapped emotion to be triggered and felt strongly.

Another well-known author, the late David Hawkins, M.D., Ph.D, mentions in his book Power vs. Force (1995) some finer details of kinesiology. Hawkins explains that kinesiology is "the intimate connection between mind and body, revealing that the mind 'thinks' with the body itself." Therefore, kinesiology (muscle testing), when used properly, can provide a avenue for the exploration of consciousness and the different dimensions of your unconscious that are difficult to fathom otherwise. Exploring the unconscious can reveal the many issues where imbalances occur between how the body and mind view experiences. Using kinesiology as a tool to tap into the subconscious not only provides access to the interconnected energy of the mind and body, but also provides an easy avenue for exploring and clearing the subconscious of resistant emotions and habitual thought forms and patterns in the form of limiting beliefs.

Disclaimer: Do not rely on muscle testing itself to determine whether you have an illness, food sensitivity or other potentially serious condition. The information in this workbook is also not intended to replace medical attention from a qualified health care professional or hospital.

Ways of Muscle Testing Yourself:

The O-ring Test

Press together the tip of your index finger and the tip of your thumb on your non-dominant hand, making an o. Saying a word that has a positive meaning for you, such as "love" or "yes," use a finger of your dominant hand, with firm but not forceful pressure, to try to pull the o apart. You can practice using five index cards with five positive statements and five negative statements and self-testing after each. Keep an open mind about what the response will be, and note what word or words consistently fail to break the connection between the pressed index finger and thumb.

Sense the opposite, subtle weakness of the thumb and index finger coming apart when saying a word that has a negative meaning for you, such as "no" or "hate." Once you practice a while and can consistently feel a difference, use those "yes" and "no" triggers as baseline words that you start every muscle testing session with. Then try using other words or phrases and sensing their higher or lower energetic frequency and how it affects your body, as indicated by outcomes of the O-ring test.

You can also consider using both hands in an O-ring position. Interlock the two o's of your thumb and index finger of both hands. Try to pull apart when you say "love" or another positive word for you, and sense the strength of the muscles. Say a negative word, such as "bitterness," and feel the weakness.

Single Finger Press

Rest the palm of one hand on a table so the hand is in a cupped position. Lifting only your index finger off the table, straighten it into the pointing position while your other fingers stay cupped on the table. Say a positive statement, such as "My name is [insert true name]," and press down firmly, but not at full strength, on the lifted index finger to see if it stays in position. Then say a statement that is false, such as "My name is Bob," and press again on the index finger. Do you notice that it has weakened? Use your baseline "yes" and "no" words or phrases to confirm what you're sensing.

If you don't have a clear sense of when the muscle test is strong versus weak with this approach, you can pull up instead of pressing down on the pointed index finger. Check to see whether the index finger stays firm and flat in relation to the table after hooking and pulling upward immediately after saying a positive word, such as "yes." See if it stays strong compared to when you say "no" or another negative word. When you get the hang of it, try practicing true and false statements, such as "I love to eat apples" and "I love to eat liver and onions" (if you dislike them), and sense the strength versus weakness of each muscle test.

Sticky Finger Muscle Test

Using your thumb and middle finger on the same hand, rub your fingers together gently and notice the smoothness of your skin between your fingers. Sense the ease of friction between your fingers while saying the word "yes" or another positive world like "love." Practice rubbing while saying a positive statement such as "I want to be well;" then while gently rubbing your fingers together, check for a friction change while saying a negative statement such as "I want to be sick." This is a great and simple way to test positive beliefs versus negative beliefs for yourself using just one hand while reading this workbook.

Tips to Self-Testing

-Drink a glass of water before starting to test; it is easy to be unaware of whether you have had enough water, and you cannot test properly when dehydrated.

-Ground yourself and meditate for 15 minutes beforehand (see approaches provided in this chapter). Meditation helps you get out of your conscious mind, which tells stories that can influence testing outcomes. Your mind needs to let go of controlling how your body responds to any statement asked of it during muscle testing.

-Start the session with a check of baseline "yes" and "no" words or statements to make sure you're ready for self-testing new statements.

-Be in a balanced emotional state for better accuracy. Just as you won't be at your best if you try to have a serious discussion with someone while furious at them, your body's responses to muscle testing can become unclear if your emotions are running rampant.

-Get neutral and don't assume you know whether a testing statement will produce a strong or weak response. That is your conscious mind acting as though it is the only voice in the room. Be in a state of allowing, like a curious child. You will receive wonderful gifts in terms of learning what your whole self believes if you act as though you are a neutral observer who is unconcerned about the outcome.

-You may have strong emotional responses to certain core issues, such as feeling unloved. A triggered state can get in the way of receiving clear responses when addressing limiting beliefs. Consider seeing a healer or health care practitioner who does muscle testing (also called applied kinesiology) to address touchy limiting beliefs. You can also seek their help to supplement the testing you do of yourself.

-One out of 20 people need a chiropractic adjustment before they will receive consistent muscle testing results. This results from their spinal energy not flowing smoothly.

Meditation and Inner-Child belief clearing

How Inner-Child Work Clears Beliefs

Your inner child is the shadow of the child you once were. We have all created limiting beliefs in each stage of our development to adulthood. Because most of our limiting beliefs come from childhood and adolescence, incorporating a healing approach that addresses unhelpful, inner-child beliefs will allow an integrated healing to occur from the innermost layers. Healing the suppressed inner child is crucial for long-term health because our inner child has stored so many memories that still impact our life today.

Every time we experience a trigger, the flood of emotions we feel causes a stress response in our immune system. Eventually this stress response from feeling triggered over and over again by a deeply ingrained limiting belief can wear the body down and we become susceptible to illness, restless sleep and fatigue. Healing this inner child is the foundation and the beginning of discovering who we are. Healing the inner child sets the stage for future healing. There is an inner-child aspect in all of us that still impacts our reaction to our environment and others.

We can learn how to rescue this inner child and be aware of the wounds of the past. Visualizing an imagined conversation with your inner child can be a great tool to navigate your way into past experiences and find the correlation between past and present problems. For example, think about a traumatic event from your childhood. Maybe another kid made fun of you and said something like, "No one likes you or wants to play with you because your too this, or too that. Go away!" As a child, you likely lacked the wisdom to consider that they were wrong. This may have caused you to create beliefs about not belonging and not being liked. If those were left unaddressed, the beliefs would continue to "talk" to you whenever others didn't include you in activities. Ask yourself, "What did I feel or think in that childhood situation?" The belief that got buried will often come to you. Once you bring such beliefs to light, you can use your favored muscle testing approach to clear them.

For many, doing work with the inner child can be as painful as it is effective. We can and should use our feeling abilities as guideposts for our limiting beliefs. Our feelings and emotions can be our guides to reveal where we are in every moment, in every situation and with every person we come into contact with. In a way emotional pain is a messenger, albeit one with teeth! You can choose to see any uncomfortable feelings as the gift that they are, or choose to avoid them and stay in repeated emotional cycles.

Childhood traumas may need to be dealt with using the aid of a mental health professional. It is never wrong to seek assistance in bettering yourself; the insight and training of a psychologist, psychiatrist or counselor can help you process whatever comes up in a healthy way. The bottom line is, you don't have to face emotionally charged limiting beliefs alone that are related to childhood or any other times in your life.

The following Inner-Child meditation was developed to uncover deep-rooted beliefs. Use this method to work beyond the lists of beliefs we have provided for you. What you uncover will be unique to you and the experiences that have shaped your life up to now. Finding and revealing those beliefs will make room for new, positive growth, and will keep you from being weighed down by your past.

Me … Meditate?

Meditation has existed for thousands of years in many different cultures throughout the world. Meditation is a powerful tool for anyone wanting to discover limiting beliefs and clear them. It works because of concentrated mental awareness. This same concentrated awareness is what is needed to find the core beliefs that are limiting you. You do not have to be a monk, a yogi or a seasoned pro to make meditation work for you. To prove this, imagine an ice cream sundae. What image comes to mind? For some it is vanilla ice cream with cherry and nuts and banana slices. For others it's the full Neapolitan with all the fixings, topped with hot fudge. If you were able to imagine a sundae just now for even a brief moment, no matter how simple it looked, then you can meditate, simple as that. Don't overthink things.

Getting Grounded

Preparing yourself for meditation is easy. Simply relax into a comfortable seated position and do a basic grounding visualization for 5 to 10 minutes. The tree root grounding technique is one we have both used to ground before our meditation practices. Close your eyes and see that, all along the length of your spine there is a tree trunk. This trunk will serve as a grounding cord, and at the base of your spine will begin the roots of the tree. Visualize long, thick roots running from the base of your spine, reaching deep into the Earth. Feel how connected and stable you have become.

As you breathe out, imagine any anxiety or stress leaving your body through these roots; they are an energy superhighway taking away your anger, worry and thoughts of your day. Continue breathing, and, with each exhale, allow the energy of your mental chatter and lists of "to dos," as well as any physical discomfort, to flow from you body, down the trunk and into the roots and the Earth. Energy flowing from you into your roots is being absorbed and dispersed this way. The Earth then cleanses this energy and sends it back up the roots whenever you inhale. The cleansed energy goes all the way to the top of your head, revitalizing and centering you.

Some people prefer lying down for meditation. A great grounding technique that fits well with this position is to imagine an umbilical cord connecting you to the Earth and rooting you to it just like the tree roots in the previous approach. If you are familiar with the energy centers in the body, you can include your chakras by imagining a cord at each chakra center that is again connected deep into the Earth. The way you ground yourself is a choice, but making grounding a habit before meditation will help you stay relaxed and clear your mind.

Inner-Child Meditation

As you are relaxing your body and mind before a meditation, randoms thoughts will likely come up and distract you. Do not worry about them; the more you focus on trying to push them away, the more they will bombard you. For particularly persistent thoughts, blow them up by postulating their energy into flowers of bubbles and pop them out of your space. Far better to acknowledge a thought as it comes up and let it go just as quickly. If it helps, you could imagine putting thoughts into a box to open up later, or see yourself blowing thoughts away like errant clouds. The more you practice meditation, the easier it will become to quiet your mind and move past the barrage of thoughts such as "Did I remember my co- worker's birthday? Is my appointment on the 25th or the 26th? I forgot to pick up milk on my way home."

Don't worry or get frustrated about such random thoughts. Instead pay attention to your breathing and use long, deep inhalations and slow, steady exhalations. Make sure you are in a comfortable position that won't cause a leg to fall asleep. You can sit or lie down, and you don't have to be cross-legged or have a perfectly straight back. As you breathe notice each part of your body, through a series of inhales and exhales. If you feel tension anywhere, let it go with your exhale.

When you are ready, imagine a nice place you have been, or have always wanted to go. The place needs to be relaxing for you—somewhere without distractions. It can be inside a building or outside in a natural setting. Go there in your mind. What smells are there? If you are outside, can you feel a light breeze? Maybe the warmth of the sun's rays as they kiss your face. Make the setting as peaceful and detailed as possible. This will be helpful in focusing your mind.

When you have your peaceful place, picture a bench there that can hold at least two people. The bench can be made of any material you would like; if the location is inside, you might want to make the bench a love seat.

Go to the bench now and take a seat. How does it feel? Is it cool to the touch or are there soft cushions covering its surface? Run your hand across the bench in the space next to where you are seated. Is it rough or smooth? Give the bench dimensions and details. Relax on your bench, soaking up the beauty of the calming surroundings. As you rest on your bench, you see someone approaching; you notice that this person looks familiar, and as this person draws closer you recognize that it is a younger version of yourself. This is your inner child. The age and appearance will vary each time you do the meditation, and it is important not to fixate on any particular age, but to just let a younger version of you appear.

Invite your inner child to join you on the bench. Feel gratitude for the insight you are about to gain. Now ask this younger self, "What limiting beliefs do I have that you want me to be aware of?" Very often you will hear an answer in the form of an actual sentence. Sometimes it might be just one word or you will see a memory from the past or another one of your senses will provide a message. If a visual memory is what comes up, just focus on what you see and later, when you finish meditating, you can write down what thoughts and memories came to you.

Pay close attention as your younger self speaks or shows you images. What feelings come up for you? What images or words flash through your mind? Be prepared for specific memories. Memories shared by your inner child can reveal the very origin of a belief for you, allowing an opportunity to clear that belief at its root. This might get uncomfortable and even a bit emotional. Allow yourself to feel the discomfort in order to heal. Sit with the emotion or memory and trust where you are led in your meditation. If you are not ready to move past a belief, it will not come up to be cleared.

When you feel that you have gained as much insight as possible from this younger version of yourself, thank your inner child for sharing. Having a feeling of gratitude will help you achieve results faster. Really feel the peace, joy and warmth of gratitude this brings. Allow your inner child to feel safe to continue to share with you in the future.

Now, when you are ready, start moving your hands and feet and bring your awareness back into the room. Write down what came up. If it was a memory, think about any limiting beliefs that likely developed from that experience. In the beginning you may only pull out one or two limiting beliefs, but with practice, you'll uncover more. We have found that usually the age of the child that comes to you is the age that particular limiting belief took hold.

Processing Belief-Clearing Information

A great way of documenting your spiritual progress is to use a journal to record your results, revisiting them as you move forward. By doing this right after sessions you can begin to recognize all the ways this work is expanding your consciousness and experiences in life. This progress report can be used with any of the clearing methods and serves as a reminder of your progression and all the layers you have peeled back. It can be very satisfying to look back over your progress and realize how much your life has changed as a result of discarding limiting beliefs. If journaling feels like a chore, consider whether you have limiting beliefs around the process of journaling and clear those limiting beliefs, such as "I am afraid to see what may come up for myself should I journal." The self-awareness activities in this workbook can be enlightening, and are meant to be at least a little fun.

Once you start clearing away old beliefs, you might notice that it takes your mind a few days, or even a few months, to recalibrate. You might find that habitual ways of thinking or feeling come up at times yet the shift allows you to experience a greater awareness. It's important to give yourself credit for noticing old thought patterns. All the new space you free up inside is going to feel a little foreign, so your brain will want to seek out something that is familiar. You can just observe these familiar thoughts now and send them on their way. No dwelling on them is required. Eventually they will not pester you regularly; in fact you might just find yourself so far removed from previous limiting beliefs that you can barely recall what the quality of those thoughts were.

Fully connecting with God/Higher Self

Every experience in your day-to-day life is an encounter that either allows you to draw closer to spirit or distances you further away, creating separation. Clearing any limiting beliefs related to your spiritual union, as discussed above and in the next chapter, is the most important activity to do if you are to be open to the flow of life, love and abundance, as well as to enjoy true health and feel true love. Clearing beliefs related to your personal ability to connect with God/Higher Self allows further and deeper healing to take place in general.

Specifically, each experience you undergo in the stages of life can become a process of internally healing judgment, hate, and old limiting beliefs. As you go through each stage, you can come to realize that those approaches are preventing you from connecting deeply. You become closer to being your loving God-self by a conscious daily awareness of your thoughts and beliefs as you heal through the process of clearing out lower frequency energies tied to hate, judgment, control, unworthiness, fear and terror. Those emotions can be replaced with loving, compassionate and forgiving beliefs.

A deeper personal connection begins in the heart, and may already be fairly developed if you are a conscious and spiritually focused individual. If so, that is wonderful, and we hope that this book will continue to strengthen and remind you of your connection. This union is an energetic and spiritual one, free from perceived blocks and barriers in our mind that result from the subconscious rumblings of limiting beliefs.

A physical body is nothing without this spiritual union, although our physical body is often all we are aware of. When there are issues affecting the spiritual body, there will be corresponding challenges that occur within the physical body. You would not be alive without your spiritual body being fully intact, and you cannot clear things in the mind or on a physical level without connecting the two.

In our combined experience of more than 18 years of practice in holistic and spiritual healing, we have seen struggles with this important interconnection manifest as significant stress related to health, life purpose, and relationship. These are the main areas where people want relief. Though it sounds like a cliché, all "big" issues and struggles that we have in our life are directly attributed to a lack of connection to God or Higher Self. The separation feeling has become an all too normal feeling that becomes . . .well normal. This is not normal however. The eternal truth is that we are first and foremost spiritual beings.

The personal connection with God/Higher Self is a oneness that is unique for every individual. Underneath every religion of this world is a desire to feel this oneness and this union consistently, eventually bringing this feeling of oneness with all into our daily experience. In our opinion, God is the love within each and every one of us. What separates us from being close to God are the shadows we project by putting too much stock on physical and behavioral differences between us. These differences, be they culturally obtained, inherited, or about race, sexual orientation or gender, mask the true oneness we share with each other. It's easier to see our differences than our similarities.

The contrasts we see are illusions separating us from ourselves and from each other. Spiritually, there are no differences between us. It should be normal for us to always feel this connection between our Higher Selves and in each other. In the spectrum of the human condition, from the wealthy to the financially poor, the heavy set to the slender and to all the colors of human skin, these illusions of difference are only present to try to heal us of the personal judgments we carry around and weigh us down. Awareness that we are judging is the beginning of healing; then healing grows as we accept that we are each in connection to the divine. The divine essence of God within us is far greater than any religious or other appearance of difference.

When limiting beliefs are consciously cleared, you become more in tune with your Higher Self, and divine nature. You can then begin to feel and know that God is everywhere—in a smile, in a hug from an old friend, in the stillness of an early morning, in the story before bedtime and in all the moments in between. God is in the mirror when we look into our own reflection and in each of the faces around us. This world we share stands a chance of becoming unified and at peace should more people recognized the human ability to connect to our higher selves and to know that God and the highest vibrations of love dwell inside all of us. Working on limiting beliefs is the first step to this unification and connection.

Within the realm of human consciousness, we each have the ability to express attributes of Christ, Mother Teresa, Buddha and other mystics. However, we can express negative aspects as well such as Stalin, Mussolini and others. The fact is that we have a choice, moment by moment, to feed the dark within us, or to feed the light. The light is the power of unconditional love of God which lies quietly within us, waiting to emerge when the veil of lower consciousness type energies and emotions are overcome and removed.

All things come down to love and fear. You are either connected to God and everyone around you, or you are disconnected from everything because of fear. It's true, hate is not the opposite of love, fear and apathy is. To create stronger connections to God/Higher Self and stay in the energy of love is to be aware of your thoughts and actions in every situation, and to ask yourself, "Am I carrying out my day-to-day actions in love or in fear? Am I making choices in life out of love or out of fear?" With just these two questions, you can learn to create healthier thoughts and patterns that will allow you to stay grounded in love, and thus create a stronger union with your Higher Self.

How do you increase your trust and connection to God/Higher Self so that all areas of your life are lived more from a place of love than from fear? Again, the answer is a simple awareness of your thoughts and beliefs concerning each area of your life so that you strive for a focus on love over fear as much as possible, and consistently act from that perspective that allows you to continue to evolve towards a higher level of consciousness.

To clarify, you are never separate from your spiritual nature. You only feel that you are because you are in a physical body and in this physical world.

It is a huge task to unlearn all the past negative thoughts and attitudes that plague our lives and cause us suffering and self-imposed limitation. Negative thoughts and feelings can never your truth. They are only the illusion. The person causing you the pain, discomfort or unease was brought to you by your own subconscious desires to heal yourself of that emotional pain, and the desire to draw closer to your true authentic self. You are drawn to people, initially often through intimate partnerships, in order to hold you in a space where healing can take place. The same can be said for every challenging circumstance that comes into your life.

Within your core is the very essence of love and of God. It is the God within you that gives intelligence to create whatever you would like to create. Your future is an accumulation of every thought you think, creating and altering your world continuously. To believe otherwise is to live life from fear-based thoughts and worn out subconscious programming that separates you from your God-self. How you clear beliefs is through connection with God, and through intention. How you get through anything is connecting with God, which will see you through challenges while having a greater awareness and perception of all that is here for your benefit to claim.

CHAPTER FOUR

LIMITING BELIEFS CONCERNING GOD AND RELIGION

"Though our feelings come and go, God's LOVE does not." C.S Lewis

The concept of God is very personal. Both of us grew up going to church and believing in a God. One of us grew up Catholic and the other a Christian. Our writing reflects the certain concepts of God that we each were raised with that led to writing some of the limiting beliefs we had on God. As you work through the beliefs in this section, simply substitute the word "God" for whichever word or deity you find most appropriate for yourself such as Higher Self, Spirit, Jesus, Buddha, Divine source, or the Universe.

The purpose of clearing beliefs about God is simple. If a person believes or feels that they are separated from God, they will seek an external source to fill that void. Often this takes the form of an addiction or a distraction. Distractions can include material possessions, risky behaviors and sometimes just mental habits that keep you running in loops. These distractions provide, if only briefly, momentary satisfaction. They hide under the masks of entertainment, food and addictions of many kinds. Escapism is just a symptom of wanting to find our authentic selves and a stronger connection to the Divine. Escapism happens under the blanket of limiting beliefs creating our illusion that we are separate from God. You feel the pull towards distractions when the void of separation takes over your life. What you feel as separation from God simply lacks light. Are you ready to step into the light?

By removing the weighted limiting beliefs, light energy will immediately come through. A shift of energy that you will actually be able to experience physically comes through your connecting to Higher Self.

We like to embrace the concept of God as adopting all positive emotions, thoughts, feelings and affirming beliefs as the frequency of God. The opposite of God and love is fear, apathy, and many words of a lower frequency. Their energy is an accumulation of negative thoughts and judgments about ourselves and God that do not serve to create a higher frequency on this planet. Simply clearing beliefs on God alone will encourage you to open up to many new possibilities.

Concerning the issue of religion, this topic can be a HUGE hot button for not only you but for the world at large. Many world religions have been turned into weapons hurled at those of other religions. Everyone is trying to prove that their religion is the most ideal. Wars have been waged on religion for milenia, and many have died for the sake of their religion. All of this animosity feeds the illusion of separation.

Religion however is not the problem. Separation and judgment upon each others' religion is. We all want to feel a connection to a Higher power. That is the underlying thread that connects us to God and that we all have in common. In a sense, no religion is good or bad. Just as the clothes people wear are different or the food we prefer is different from culture to culture, or one neighborhood to the next, it's the way we desire to personally serve God or connect to a higher power is different, yet it has the same goal in mind. That end goal we all seek is to connect to the same source, a higher power which is love.

Limiting beliefs concerning God and religion that you can clear:

God cannot be trusted.
My belief in God is conditional upon him meeting my expectations.
I cannot depend on God/religions.
I cannot now, nor will I ever accept the existence of God.
I am skeptical God exists.
I am skeptical God will love me when I sin by .
I deny and discard the concept of God.
The concept of God is too much for me to accept.
God is a Lie/liar.
God is not real.
God is made up to control people.
In order to believe in God one must be religious.
I should not and cannot trust God.
There is an impenetrable barrier between myself and God.
There is no God.
God is dead.
God hates people.
God will destroy what I create.
God will destroy me.
God is angry with me.
God is not safe.
It is not safe for me to love God.
God does not want my goals desire and dreams to come easy.
God will sabotage me.
I have no faith in God or higher power.
God is false.
God wants me to be broken.
God wants me to have limits.
God wants me to fail so I can learn.
God does not want me to have inner peace because I have not earned it.

I must fear God.

God keeps score and I am losing.

The concept of God is ridiculous and impossible.

God never wants me to be happy.

God is vengeful.

I am forsaken by God

I am abandoned by God

God finds fault in me.

God sees that I am a loser.

God is not even aware of me or my needs.

God never listens to me.

My prayers are not important to God.

It is selfish of me to expect miracles from the Divine to happen in my life.

God works miracles in the live of others, but not me.

Taking time to recharge and relax is forbidden by God.

Having the life I want is forbidden by God.

God values others over me.

I am a disappointment to God.

If I put my faith in God he will disappoint me.

To believe in God is to believe in fairytales.

The idea of God is a nice story, but that is all he is...a story.

God does not want me.

I have failed God and will never be accepted.

I am resentful and angry with God.

God thinks I'm a loser.

I cannot open my heart to God.

It is not safe to open my heart to God.

God thinks women are less important than men.

God thinks women are not as smart as men.

God loves men more than woman.

God loves women more than men.

God does not want me to feel safe and secure.

God will expose me for my faults.

God thinks new cars are useless.

God does not want life to be easy for me.

God thinks I am a fraud.

God does not want me, I am alone.

God wants me to hate myself.

God hates me.

God wants me think I am not worth loving.

God does not want me.

God wants me to do everything myself and not ask for help.

God does not want me to have fun.

God does not want me to be totally clear.

God wants me to be in fear.

God wants me to be punished first before I gain my spiritual insight/creativity.

God will abandon me.

God has doomed me to a life of boredom, sadness, regret.

I cannot accept God's love for me.

I feel guilty for believing to have separated from God.

I cannot tolerate religion.

I am not able to tolerate religious people.

Going to church is the only way to serve God.

It is impossible for me to believe in God.

It is impossible for God to believe in me.

God will punish me if I make mistakes.

God hates me if I make mistakes.

God blames me if I make mistakes.

God thinks it is selfish of me to pursue my dreams and goals.

God wants me/needs me to work hard.

I doubt God's love for me.

I will never be connected fully to God.

I am separate from God.

God doesn't want me to have what I want.

God judges me.

God thinks I am a failure.

I have failed God.

God does not want me.

God does not want me to achieve success and abundance.

God does not want me to achieve .

God wants me to be in control of everything all the time.

God will punish me if I forget anything.

God thinks I am worthless.

God thinks I deserve pain and suffering.

God thinks I don't deserve good things.

God will never forgive me.

I have abandoned God and will never be forgiven.

God has given up on me.

God has taken so much from me.

I cannot forgive God.

I am unwilling to give God permission to love me despite my sin of .

I cannot forgive myself for hating God.

God allows bad things to happen to me.

God does not want me to be completely well.

God allows bad things to happen to good people.

I cannot let go of my anger and fear toward God.

God knows I am not good enough.

God tortures me.

I am tormented because God wants it.

I desire torment and pain to be pure for God.

God does not want me healed.

God needs me to suffer for him.

God has cast me out.

I have done something that only God must forgive me for.

My pain and lack serves God.

God has no faith in me.

God will not love me if I am anything less than perfect.

I have to give to others to the point of exhaustion so God will love me.

God will only love me if I am free from sin.

God wants me to stay in debt in order to learn.

God doesn't want me to be wealthy.

God wants me to believe that I need to sabotage myself in order to be closer to him.

God expects me to suffer for him.

God will punish me if I am successful.

God wants me to be punished.

God wants me to be in emotional pain

God wants me to hold onto limitations and lack.

God is too busy for me.

God is angry with me and withholding his love.

God doesn't love me unconditionally.

God does not want me to be close to people.

It is not not possible for me to be closer to God because of my sin.

It is not possible for me to be closer to God because of my (greed, addiction, anger, deceit, etc.)

God does not want me.

God places limits on my abilities

God places limits on my energy.

God does not want good things in life to come easy.

God does not want me to have success.

God does not want me to be happy.

I am repulsive to God.

There is no use, God will never accept me.

I should be punished by God.

I want to be punished by God for my sins.

God will take away everyone I love.

Wealth, success and fortune will separate me further from God.

God wants to hurt me.

God does not want me to have a lot of money.

God thinks money is evil.

God knows money will corrupt me.

God thinks I am evil.

I am evil because I have sinned against God.

God does not want me to feel good about myself.

As a child I had the concept of a vengeful God forced upon me, I want no part of God now.

God does not want me to be attractive.

God will hate me if I get what I want.

God holds me back.

God prevents me from getting what I want in life.

God doesn't want me to spend money or time on myself.

God does not want me to spend money on things I want.

I am not capable of believing in God.

I am not capable of believing in God.

I am not capable of loving God.

God is not capable of loving me because I have sinned.

God does not want me to have nice things, love or security in my life.

God will judge and punish you when you are bad.

Where is God when I need him?

There isn't a God that really cares.

Asking for God's help is selfish.

I am selfish for wanting help from divinity.

If God sees my willingness to fight for what I need and want, I will be rewarded.

If I don't work hard to be better God will never let me have what I want.

God wants me to work when I am around people.

God sees me as unclean.

God will smite me.

God will kill me.

God despises me.

God sees me only as a sinner.

Life is lack, loving and believing in God will not change that.

God does not want me to be loved by anyone.

God is angry with me for my past.

It is a fact that God is displeased with me.

God has taken so much from me that I cannot forgive.

I have sinned so much that I should not even forgive myself.

My misery is God's fault therefore I want no part of God.

It is a fact that God does not exist.

God cannot exist.

God may exist for others but not for me.

I rely on my beliefs that there is no God in order to feel safe.

I rely on my limiting beliefs about God to be accepted by my peers/colleagues.

The group of people I am a part of would never accept or understand me believing in God.

It is a fact that I have failed God and will never be forgiven.

It is a fact that I am to live a life of suffering in order to prove to God that I am worthy.

Divine assistance is only for others not me.

God expects me to handle everything alone.

If I appear weak to God I will be punished.

Asking for God's help makes me weak.

God wants me to put others needs before me own always.

God created me to suffer.

I am to suffer for God.

God's love has conditions.

It is impossible to let go of my anger towards God.

It is impossible for God to love or accept me as I am.

It's too much for me to handle to form new beliefs about God.

I am too flawed for God to love or accept.

Changing my mind or beliefs about God will bring nothing but disappointment.

There is no part of me that is God.

I can't be a part of God.

There is an impenetrable barrier between myself and God.

I will never be able to see in myself what God sees in me.

God sees my suffering and does nothing to stop it.

God sees the suffering of the world and does nothing to stop it.

God allows me to suffer.

God expects people to take advantage of me.

God wants me in poverty to prove my worthiness.

I must choose between God and being happy.

I must choose between God and security and abundance.

I must choose between God and money/ wealth.

I must choose between God and my health.

Because I must choose between God and being happy, I have to stay stuck where I am.

God wants me to be taken advantage of in order to learn my lessons.

God prevents me from clearing my limiting beliefs.

If I clear my limiting beliefs God will find more work for me to do.

Because I am female/male I will not be accepted by God.

It is hard to be accepted by God.

God finds me lacking and does not want to work through me.

God does not want me to be without pain.

God does not want me to be pain free.

My pain is my way of proving myself to God.

My limited life is my way of proving myself to God.

I am too insignificant to matter to God.

I am not important enough for God to bother with.

God has bigger things than me to care about.

Other people and issues far more important to God than I am.

The rules I make myself live by are a way of proving myself worthy of God's acceptance and love.

If I make mistakes God will not be pleased.

If I allow a better way of life to happen for me God will hate me.

If I accept money for my work God will hate me.

I can never do enough to please God.

My past mistakes prevent me from having God's love or forgiveness.

I will never see myself as a God does.

I will never see the world as God sees it.

I will never see others the way God does.

God wants to keep me uninspired.

I am incapable of acting as a God acts.

I will never be the recipient of God's work in my life.

I will never think as God thinks.

I will never hear as God hears.

I will never connect fully to God.

I will never be clean enough for God.

If I live the life I truly want I will end up failing God.

It is better for me to stay in fear of God.

I will never be free from limiting beliefs about God.

My religion has taught me that I am unclean and in need of forgiveness.

If I clear beliefs concerning God, then I am committing a sin.

My religious beliefs are the only right beliefs.

All other religions are wrong.

It is a sin for me to have a more expensive concept of God.

God will turn against me if I decide my religion is no longer what I need to grow.

I owe my life to serve only the concept of God that my religion teaches.

I am not religious so I will not be saved.

My past was so egregious that I can only be saved by religion.

I cannot be saved unless I punish myself.

I require being saved by God.

I will never get into heaven.

My religion is the only way to get into heaven.

I have no faith in myself.

God has no faith in me.

It's normal for me to feel neglected by God.

God has no faith in me because of my own self loathing.

God has no faith in me because I am untrustworthy.

If I change my mind about my faith I will be seen as a hypocrite.

Because I doubt my own goodness I am not worthy of God's love.

I am not acceptable to God.

Because of my past I cannot be a part of God.

My environment has taught me there is separation from God, and others.

Positive belief Affirmations to help bring neutrality towards God:

I am a part of God.

I know how to be a part of God.

I am worthy of God's love no matter what.

God loves me for who I am.

God is on my side.

God is my co-partner in life.

God is a co-creator in my life.

I know how to live my life without feeling neglected by God.

God's love is unconditional.

I have the divine right to be connected to God at all times.

I give myself permission to be connected to God at all times.

I give myself permission to believe in God and to know God believes in me.

I know how it feels to have faith in God and in myself.

I give myself permission to accept having faith in God and myself.

I know how to live without feeling separate from God.

There is no separation between myself and God.

I know what it feels like to be loved unconditionally by God.

I know how to feel supported by God and the universe.

I deserve God's love.

I am worthy of God's love.

God sees me as worthy and deserving of love.

I am not defined by my mistakes.

I have nothing to prove to God.

I completely accept a more expanded concept of God.

I accept the concept of God being a part of me and me being a part of God.

I allow my heart and mind to be in harmony with an expanded concept of God.

If I ask for Divine assistance it will come.

It is easy for me to see God at work in my life.

It is easy for me to see Divinity at work in my life.

I am ready to receive all the positive benefits of allowing a closer connection to God.

My faith in God and his willingness to work miracles in my life is strong.

I accept all of the good into my life that God has been waiting patiently to give me.

God's love for me knows no boundaries.

God see me and accepts me just as I am.

I allow an expanded concept of faith into my daily experiences.

I release all of my barriers to faith.

I have no need for boundaries from faith.

I fully accept with all my faith the gifts God has given me.

I have faith in the direction my life will go.

I have faith that God will provide me with all that I want or need.

I am willing to receive all the benefits of having faith that God will provide me with all that I need.

I never miss an opportunity from Divinity.

I have faith in Divine timing and know how to be patient.

I can be a member of my church and have a unique perspective of God.

It is okay for me to have different ideas about God from those I was raised with.

I do know what it is like to have faith that I am fully supported by God.

I am able to give up control and surrender my struggle to God.

Mayline Robertson and Nicole Biondich

Journaling To solidify what you have learned

How has your beliefs concerning God limited your faith?

_____

_____

_____

_____

_____

_____

What areas of your life have opened up now that you cleared beliefs on your perception of God?

_____

_____

_____

_____

_____

_____

CHAPTER FIVE

ELIMINATING SEPARATION, SUFFERING AND SACRIFICE

"Suffering is a great teacher and you never know what it might teach you once you work through it." -Bryant McGill

Stepping into Wholeness

Separation beliefs ultimately relate to feeling separate from God and love. It is difficult to avoid negative mentions on the news, or people with disparaging remarks about different groups which foster a feeling of being separate or different from others. These beliefs keep us in a state of disconnect where we see ourselves as separate from each other. This separation often results from being exposed to religious doctrines that state that we must work in order to connect to God. The feeling that you are separate from others all derive from the same place – a disconnect from the God/Love/Higher Self that is in each of us.

The good news about this interrelatedness is that clearing any separation beliefs you have will help you three times over; doing so will help you clear the feeling that you are separate from God, from others, and from yourself. It is only our beliefs that keep us in a state of judgment, hate, and intolerance, and therefore, separate from each other and from our true loving nature of God.

Being of different races and religions should enrich our lives, not keep us feeling more distant. By believing that our particular faith or way to worship or connect to God is above somebody else's we feed the illusion of separation; in truth, we all want the same connection.

As you pay more attention to your beliefs, you become more aware that you may have judgmental thoughts concerning certain religion or race of people. You may recognize this separation as feelings of being uneasy, uncomfortable or of even wanting to avoid reading about certain ideas or hanging out with certain people. The process of paying more attention to your thoughts may also trigger inherited beliefs that you didn't even know you had. Being judgmental doesn't serve anyone, and you can choose to become part of the world-wide movement of finally waking up to sensing this divisive energy and actually doing something about it.

We are including beliefs below about separation from one another that focuses on judgments about race, gender and religion because they are so common. We have also found that many clients have multiple prejudices against people of certain religions, professions, gender identities, weights, and ages.

When we see something in another that we find unacceptable or undesirable, what we reject is often not about that person. We are often reacting to an aspect within ourselves that we find uncomfortable sensing when that judgment is mirrored back to us and seeing ourselves in full light. Judgement as a buried belief is what triggers the anger or uneasiness within ourselves. These triggers can be very personal, so we have left blank lines on some of these so that you can add in your own specific beliefs.

Some limiting beliefs you could remove that are related to separation, suffering and sacrifice include:

I am separate from my dreams.

Every day is filled with separation from God.

I vow to remain separate from others and God.

My sickness separates me from God and happiness.

The color of my skin separates me from others.

God conspires against me to keep me separate from my dreams.

I have no faith because all I see is suffering.

Judgment of myself separates me from my goals.

I am separate from abundance.

I am separate from my family and friends.

I don't deserve to be connected to God and all the good.

I am not worthy enough to be connected to God.

Because I am human, I must be separate from God.

I want to be separate from everyone because I am different.

I'm a mistake.

I don't belong anywhere.

I see myself separate from other ethnicities.

My friend's see me separate from them.

No one can see all my separate identities.

It's not safe for everyone to see all my separate identities.

Because I have human desires, I am separate from God.

Because I have human weaknesses, I am separate from God.

I have sinned; therefore, I am forever separate from God.

Being separate from the abundance of life is normal for me.

Being separate from the abundance of self love is normal for me.

It is possible for other people to be connected to God, but I must remain separate.

Being separated from God feels normal to me.

I enjoy being separate from God.

There is no point in clearing separation beliefs.

Separation from God and others is my only reality.

I am not good enough to be a part of God.

I see myself as different from others.

The world sees me as different, and therefore separate from them.

My family sees me as separate from them.

I need to work hard in order to not feel separated from God.

Wealth, success, and fortune will separate me further from God.

I need to fill the void from feeling separate from God.

I feel punished by God because of my belief that I have separated from him through my desires.

I want to be separate from God.

I deserve to be separate from God.

Because of the emptiness I feel, I am separated from God and my Higher Self.

Because of the emptiness I carry, I am separated from Love.

I fill my time with distractions in order to fill the emptiness.

I fill the emptiness with addictions.

The burden of my addictions separates me from love.

The darkness in my soul separates me from Love/God/Higher Self.

I am lost and broken, and therefore separated from God.

If I do not suffer, then I am not interesting.

All creative people must suffer for their art.

I must suffer and work hard in order to have a good life.

If I do not suffer, then I cannot relate to others.

All I see is suffering all around me.

The environment is suffering.

I feel guilty for having a good life free from suffering.

I cause the suffering of others.

It is my life purpose to suffer.

I prove how strong I am by enduring struggle.

I prove how strong I am by pushing through struggle.

I prove my worthiness by enduring suffering.

I get my attention by enduring suffering.

I am only worthy if I suffer.

Suffering keeps the world from seeing my failure.

I create suffering so I know who will love and support me.

I only get loved when I suffer or struggle.

I only get attention when I suffer or struggle.

I only get attention from myself when I suffer.

I do not have the right to be free from suffering.

I must suffer in order to feel secure in life.

Suffering and hard work will get me a place in heaven.

Suffering is the only way to get to heaven.

I wish to suffer.

I cannot allow God to provide for me.

I have to inflict pain upon myself in order to feel love from myself, others, and God.

I need to deprive myself of things I want or need in order to be loved by God.

Needing help is a sign of weakness.

I must suffer through this life to accomplish what I came here to learn.

If I am not suffering, I am not growing.

If I do not struggle I am not being good.

I cannot give myself permission to release suffering and struggle from my life.

The hole in me will never be filled.

There is no point in clearing suffering beliefs.

There is no point in clearing beliefs about struggle.

I will always struggle with .

Holding on to limitations serves me in some way.

Holding on to suffering serves me in some way.

Suffering equals strength and knowledge.

Suffering is and will always be my path.

Suffering is just how life is.

I have to suffer in order to succeed.

I have to suffer in order to be happy.

Nothing in life comes without suffering.

Nothing good in life comes without suffering.

I need to suffer in order to be good at anything.

If I punish myself and suffer, I will no longer be separate from God/Higher Self.

I must suffer for past mistakes and past choices.

I enjoy suffering.

I don't know how to stop suffering.

I do not know how to live without wanting to suffer.

I must suffer and be separate from God/Higher Self because of my past choices.

I do not measure up to God's expectations; therefore, I must suffer.

I want to suffer.

I deserve to suffer.

I live daily with suffering.

I live daily with pain both emotional and physical.

My life is a hopeless struggle filled with suffering and pain.

Misery, pain and failure are my only reality.

I am doomed to a life of suffering.

I cannot give myself permission to release suffering.

Pain and suffering are my penance.

Pain and suffering are the only reality possible for me.

Pain and suffering are all that I deserve to experience.

Struggle, separation, and pain is my reality.

I live a life of struggle, pain, lack, suffering and separation.

I cannot give up the fight.

If I don't fight, someone else will win.

No one else will fight for me.

I have to fight in order to win.

I have to fight to live.

Fighting to survive or struggle is what makes me a good person.

It is not safe to give up the fight.

Life is a constant battle.

It is impossible to achieve anything without fighting and struggling for it.

Freedom from pain, suffering, and separation is impossible.

I do not deserve to be free from pain, suffering, fighting to survive, and separation.

I have to fight to survive.

I fight and struggle for everything I have.

I will not know who I am without struggle, pain, suffering, and separation.

Without pain and suffering, I will feel nothing.

My suffering is not complete.

Pain equals depth.

I deserve pain.

I desire pain.

I enjoy pain.

I am accomplishing something if I am in pain.

I desire struggle, suffering, and separation.

I desire to fight to survive.

I have to let people take advantage of me.

I attract suffering and pain.

I attract people who cause me suffering and pain.

I attract people who want to take advantage of me.

I have too many blocks to freedom from pain, suffering, separation, and struggle to ever be clear.

In order to be accountable, I must be punished.

In order for others to see me as accountable, I must be punished.

I have to be held accountable.

I will never get ahead.

I am not capable of releasing my desire to suffer.

Suffering makes me a stronger, capable, and respectable person.

If I fail the world, then I am of no value to God.

It's wrong to ask God for too much.

It's wrong to ask God for help.

God does not love me because I have done terrible things.

Life has to be full of struggle/suffering.

I am meant to take on everyone's pain and suffering.

The more I suffer, the closer I am to God/Higher Self.

I get my value from suffering.

I see that others suffer, and I cannot allow myself to be free when they are not.

God will punish me if I give up fighting to survive, pain, suffering, struggle and being separate from him.

I am doomed to a life of fighting to survive, pain, struggle, suffering, and being separate from God/ Higher Self.

Life is about fighting to survive, pain, suffering, struggle and being separate from God/ Higher Self.

I can never allow myself to clear pain, suffering, fighting to survive, struggle or separation from my life.

I don't have what it takes to release pain, struggle, suffering, fighting to survive, and being separate from God/Higher Self.

I must experience suffering, struggle, pain, and separation in order to grow.

Struggle, suffering, fighting to survive, pain, and separation from God/Higher Self is my identity.

It is unnatural to be free from suffering, pain, struggle, and separation.

Suffering, pain, struggle, and separation are what feeds my soul.

I must earn joy through suffering, struggle, fighting to survive, pain, and separation.

It is a sin to want to be free from suffering, pain, struggle, and separation.

Life is hard.

Life is painful to get through.

Life is a struggle.

Life is cruel.

Life is unfair.

Life is meant to be difficult.

Life is an uphill battle.

My life is a hopeless struggle.

My life will never be filled with joy and incredible experiences.

My life is only filled with pain and suffering.

Every day is filled with pain, suffering, fighting, regret, struggle, separation, and depression.

I do not have what it takes to make a great life for myself.

I must suffer so that others can be free from pain.

I must shoulder all the pain and suffering in all the world.

I will always hurt, physically and emotionally.

I will always have to struggle and fight to survive.

I must experience pain and suffering in order to gain clarity.

I must fight to survive in order to grow.

I must be in emotional pain in order to grow.

No pain, no gain.

God gives me strength only to be able to suffer for him.

I am terrified that suffering is needed in order to feel my unexpressed emotions.

Life is meant to be difficult.

You do not grow as much from joy as you do from suffering.

You do not learn as much from joy as you do from suffering.

Joy is not my reality.

Joy is not meant for me.

It is unnatural to attend to my own needs first.

We are all made to suffer.

Fighting to survive feeds my soul.

I have depth because I suffer.

Suffering is truth.

Suffering is reality.

I am not a real man/woman unless I suffer.

Life is meant to be difficult.

I have not done enough to earn joy.

I have to suffer in order to be loved.

I need to suffer in order to be able to love myself.

I must suffer so others will not.

I must sacrifice myself for others.

If I am free from suffering, my friends and family will be jealous.

I have to suffer in order to be creative.

All creative and interesting people suffer from depression, and if I want to be creative and interesting, I must be depressed too.

If I am to be creative and interesting, I have to suffer and be wounded.

It is a sin to want to be free from having to fight to survive.

I cannot help others unless I am suffering.

I must suffer in order to heal others.

People of the race deserved to suffer and are separate from me and God.

People of the religion deserve to suffer and are separate from me and from God.

Because I am part of the race, I must suffer.

Because I am part of the human race, I deserve to suffer.

The human race is separate from God.

The human race must suffer, struggle, be in pain, and fight to survive.

Because I am part of the religion, I have to fight to survive.

Because I am part of the race, I have to fight to survive.

Because I am part of the race, I am weak.

Because I am, I am separate from other people.

Lawyers deserve to suffer and are separate from me and from God.

Bankers deserve to suffer and are separate from me and from God.

People who are paid for sex deserve to suffer and are separate from me and from God.

Addicts deserve to suffer and are separate from me and from God.

People who are gay or lesbian deserve to suffer and are separate from me and from God.

People who are straight deserve to suffer and are separate from me and from God.

Salesmen deserve to suffer and are separate from me and from God.

Women/Men deserve to suffer and are separate from me and from God.

Suffering, hard work, fighting to survive, pain, and struggle will earn me a place in heaven.

I am not capable of releasing my intolerance for .

People of religion are not perfect.

People of race are not perfect.

Young people deserve to suffer and fight to survive.

Young people deserve to suffer so that they can figure things out.

Young people are separate from me and from God.

Old people are separate from me and from God.

I cannot allow the good God wants for me to enter my life because I am flawed. (insert your own adjective)

I have not suffered enough.

I vow to suffer, struggle, and experience pain.

God believes I have not suffered enough.

I vow to always have to fight to survive.

Because I hate myself, I need to continue to suffer.

I must sacrifice time with my loved ones in order to be successful.

I have to sacrifice my happiness in order to have stability and security in my life.

I have to sacrifice my happiness for that of my children/family/partner.

I have to sacrifice my happiness for . (specific person)

My parents sacrificed for me, so I must honor them by sacrificing too.

I must sacrifice my voice so that others can have theirs.

Everyone sacrifices something; why should I not have to?

I must sacrifice my happiness to prove to others that I am worthy.

Achieving anything without sacrifice is no real achievement.

Society, my family and God expect me to sacrifice.

I have to sacrifice my time to others.

I have to sacrifice my money/time for others.

I have to sacrifice my values for my relationship.

I have to sacrifice my freedom for my job/relationship.

I only allow myself to feel good about me if I sacrifice everything for others.

Because people I love are suffering, I must sacrifice my happiness to care for them.

I am expected to sacrifice for others.

I can never sacrifice enough to earn my happiness/freedom.

I sacrifice my financial security to help my children to prove I love them. (Insert your relationship)

I sacrifice my dreams and goals so that others can achieve theirs.

There is only so much joy and happiness to go around, so I will go without.

I am not worthy of joy and happiness.

I would rather suffer than face my inner emptiness.

I would rather escape my life than face my failure.

A life of emptiness is all I know.

I cant withstand facing the emptiness when I feel .

I must always run away from the emptiness that I feel in order to live.

Escaping the emptiness I feel is all that I know.

I can't enjoy life because I always feel so empty.

Because of the emptiness I carry, I can never enjoy life.

Because of the emptiness I feel, nothing is worth living for.

The emptiness inside causes me to feel alone.

I must escape by any means possible rather than face aloneness.

Without faith in myself and others I feel empty.

I have no faith; therefore, I will suffer.

I have no faith that life will get better for me.

I cannot escape the emptiness I feel.

The emptiness I feel causes me to feel panic.

The emptiness I feel causes me to be overwhelmed.

I feel empty when life isn't what I expected it to be.

I feel empty because life has disappointed me.

I feel empty because my relationships disappoint me.

The emptiness I feel doesn't allow me to be happy.

Without planning my future, I feel empty.

I need to punish myself in order to avoid the emptiness I feel.

I have to avoid the emptiness I feel by self-destructive behaviors.

Without maintaining my current self-image, I feel empty.

I feel empty without a need to worry about future security.

Because I am in a position of leadership, I must sacrifice for others.

You can't have everything.

I won't allow myself to achieve my goals without sacrifice.

I can have peace or I can have security, but I cannot have both.

I can have time or I can have money, but I can't have both.

I can be happy or I can be free, but I cannot be both.

I can be successful or I can be happy, but I cannot be both.

I can be safe or I can be free, but I can't be both.

I cannot have everything I want or need because others will be jealous.

My destructive behaviors are stronger than my personal power to overcome them.

My environment has taught my that I will experience lack, struggle, suffering and sacrifice.

Nothing exists after death. (Remember that not every statement applies to every reader, and clear for this belief if it feels limiting to you.)

Death is painful.

Death is the end, and separates people from those they love.

Select from among these positive belief affirmations that you could tap in:

I know how to evolve spiritually free from suffering and free from feeling separate from God.

I can be close to God/Higher Self free from suffering.

I can be close to others free from suffering.

I have awakened from the illusion of suffering.

I can experience life free from emotional pain.

I can experience life free from physical pain.

There are no barriers between myself and God.

I am one with God and all of creation.

I am whole.

I am connected to God despite my human limitations.

I am connected to God despite my human weaknesses.

I can live a life without emptiness.

I give myself permission to live a life without emptiness.

I am safe without barriers between myself and others.

I am safe without barriers between myself and God.

My life is blessed with positive energies only.

God loves me and blesses me.

There is an abundance of love within my life.

I know how to think with Love.

I can allow myself to always think with Love.

I know how to think with love towards myself and others.

I know what it feels like to be one with God/Higher Self.

I am respecting and supporting myself daily.

There is only peace, as I am connected to God/Higher Self.

Experiences are meant to help me grow, not to break me.

My life has value, and I have the confidence and understanding to develop healthy relationships.

I release any self-defeating desires that are separating me from God/Higher Self.

I allow myself to feel connected to God, my Higher Self and others.

I release all desire of feeling ashamed for having felt separated from God/Higher Self.

I give myself permission to enjoy life without feeling separate from God/Higher Self.

I give myself permission to release all feelings of regret concerning addictions and life choices that make me feel separate from God/Higher Self.

I release all desires that make me feel separate from God.

I release all feelings of shame for feeling separated from God due to my addictions.

I release my fears of going out into the world that lead me to feel I am separate from God.

I release my insecurities in relationships that lead me to feel I am separate from God/Higher Self.

I release all feelings of not being enough that lead me to feel separate from God/ Higher Self.

I release all feelings of self-doubt that lead me to feel separate from God/Higher Self.

I release all feelings of lack of confidence that lead me to feel separate from God/ Higher Self.

I release all feelings of not belonging that lead me to feel separate from God/Higher Self.

I release all feelings that I have disappointed God that lead me to feeling separate from him.

I release all doubts, feelings, and beliefs that God will not take care of me or provide for me.

I release all feelings of low self-worth that lead me to feeling I am separate from God/Higher Self.

I deserve to be free of suffering and struggle.

I deserve a life free from emptiness.

I deserve to enjoy a perfect life.

I am worth enough to enjoy a perfect life.

I deserve to feel whole and connected to God/Higher Self.

I know how to help others without sacrificing my own well-being.

I know how to achieve my dreams and goals without sacrificing everything.

I can have both happiness and success.

I can have both happiness and time.

It is not necessary to sacrifice myself to prove my worth.

I can experience death without pain or suffering.

I have awakened from the illusion of separation from God.

I have awakened from the illusion of being separate from other people.

I have awakened from the illusion of being separate from my High Self.

Journaling to solidify what you have learned

In what areas of your life have you felt separation?

In what ways have you felt more connected since clearing separation, suffering or sacrifice-related beliefs?

_____

_____

_____

_____

_____

_____

_____

After working through this chapter, what new ideas do you have have concerning separation in your own life? Do you feel separate from yourself? Your Higher Self? Your family? Create your own specific beliefs on your particular area you feel blocked or separated from.

_____

_____

_____

_____

_____

_____

_____

CHAPTER SIX

ELIMINATING UNWORTHINESS AND FAILURE

"No one can set your level of worthiness except you."
-Bryant Mcgill

Uncovering Your True Worth

Every one of us has experienced, at one time or another, the feeling of being unworthy. Aside from our physical needs as a child, we each have many emotional needs that require attention in order to grow up feeling worthy. Experiencing love, affection, and approval from our parents and family would encourage our feelings of worthiness. When these emotional needs are not provided for, people develop the tendency to believe they weren't worthy of them. Later on, this lack of emotional support can result in reacting to moments when life doesn't go your way. Listening to the whispers of unworthiness remind you of your shortcomings. Sometimes feelings of unworthiness SHOUTS at you so loudly, it can freeze you in your tracks and keep you from pursuing your dreams.

The range of expressions of unworthiness can permeate every facet of life, making it hard to accept the goodness life has to offer. Negative patterns such as addiction can result as byproducts of the many belief forms of unworthiness, betraying you into believing that you have little value. When you base your self-worth on how negative events play out, you continue to foster those unworthy beliefs.

Even for those who strive to overcome every feeling of being "less than" while seeking to meet all of society's impossible standards, the stress and worry of constantly needing to keep up can be exhausting. Carrying around so many beliefs blocking your ability to feel worthy of the good things in life can thus keep you from reaching for a life that would truly bring happiness to you.

What would your life be like if you knew without a doubt that you were worthy of abundance and peace, and had value beyond measure? How do you think your relationships would change? Experiencing a knowingness of your worthiness sets you free in many ways that can be unexpected. Life's challenges become easier to work with and relationships become more effortless when you know you are worthy to accept life's abundance. In addition, your heart will become more open to receiving self love when you acknowledge self-worth and are able to love others more fully as well.

Here are some beliefs you can clear related to unworthiness:

My worth is determined by the opinions of others.
I don't know who I am or who I want to be.
If I stay unworthy, less is expected of me.
If I free myself from being unworthy, I'll have to be responsible.
I become who you want me to be to avoid contention.
It is my identity to be unworthy.

People of religion are unworthy.

People of race are unworthy.

People who do __for a profession are unworthy.

Because I am, I am unworthy.

I will not give myself permission to feel worthy.

I cannot give myself permission to feel worthy.

I am unworthy of love, acceptance, peace, and abundance.

I vow to remain unworthy.

Feeling worthy is impossible.

Being worthy is impossible.

Because I have sinned, I am unworthy.

I can't get better or smarter.

I'm not worthy enough to be happy or healthy.

I'm not worthy enough to be successful.

God does not believe I am worthy enough.

I will never believe in my own worth.

I have no worth beyond what others think of me.

I get my self-worth belonging to a certain group of people.

I'm afraid I'm not good enough.

I'm afraid I'll never be good enough.

I can never be happy because my expectations of myself are too high.

I can never be successful because my expectations of myself are too high.

I'm afraid of facing my true authentic self.

I'm afraid I'm not good enough because I'm not worthy.

I underachieve so I don't make others look bad.

I diminish my own accomplishments in order to not be egotistical.

I'm not good enough because I'm not worthy of love.

I have to continue to keep doing things until I make myself worthy.

If I don't make a certain amount of money, I am not worthy.

I'm not worthy to meet the perfect person.

I'm not worthy of forgiveness.

God will not allow me to feel worthy.

It's shameful to avoid work and responsibility.

I will always allow to make me feel unworthy.

Without a relationship, I am not worthy.

Without a purpose, I am not worthy.

Without a job, I am not worthy.

No matter how much I try, I am not worthy or enough.

Because I struggle with an addiction, I am not worthy.

I must deflect my own feelings of inadequacy by putting down or judging others.

I distract myself from my responsibilities because I feel unworthy.

If I'm good I'll be rewarded, and if I'm bad I'll be punished.

I have something to prove in life.

I'm not good enough because I've done terrible things.

I'm not good enough because I have sinned.

I have to be sinless in order to feel worthy.

I am not worthy because my spouse left me for another person.

I'm not good enough because I'm flawed.

I'm not good enough because I'm limited by my imperfections.

I can't receive love because I'm not good enough and not worthy.

My past mistakes block me from receiving God's love.

If God really loved me, I wouldn't be suffering like this.

Others' opinions of me is of great importance.

It matters a great deal that other people think I am good enough.

I must care about what other people think of me. (for all teenagers)

I am not perfect just as I am.

I am imperfect.

I am not comfortable in my own skin.

If it's perfect, nothing can go wrong.

I am not worth loving.

I have to perceive myself in a certain way in order to feel safe.

My perception of myself isn't as important as others' perceptions of me.

My perception of myself and others are in conflict.

Being competitive feeds my worthiness.

I must be competitive in order to feel worthy.

I must be perfect in order to feel worthy.

I'm unworthy because I chose a career over being a parent.

If I can't sacrifice for others I'll be seen as unworthy.

I can't receive love because I'm not worthy of it.

I need to be codependent on somebody in order to avoid feeling unworthy.

I need to be codependent on someone else's drama to avoid feeling unworthy.

You can tap in some of these affirmations about worthiness to replace previous unworthiness beliefs:

I can feel important without others' approval.

I am balancing my life, and I know when good is good enough.

I can be successful despite the expectations I place upon myself.

I can have a healthy perception of myself despite others' opinions.

I am worthy of God's love.

I am worthy of my families love.

I am worthy of a healthy relationship.

I am worthy of experiencing all the good things in life and in love.

I am worthy enough to be treated right.

I am worthy of abundance despite the poverty I came from.

I give myself permission to feel worthy of all good things.

I am worthy despite my failures.

I am worthy to be accepted by God.

I am worthy to have the work and purpose that I choose for myself.

I am worthy of having time for myself.

I know how to live my life feeling worthy of all positive things.

I am worthy of self-love.

I am worthy of a better life.

I am worthy of embracing my inner guidance.

I give myself permission to release all feelings of unworthiness that are separating me from God and life.

It is normal for me to feel confident and worthy.

It is normal for me to attract only people who know my worth and treat me well.

In addition to clearing unworthiness beliefs, it is important not to waste time punishing yourself for what you think you may have missed out on from feeling unworthy. Instead, take comfort in knowing that you have taken a major step forward in the right direction by building the life that you have always been worthy of. Replacing your unworthiness beliefs with positive belief affirmations you will be blown away by how much you can create and be validated in your own self-worth by what begins to unfold for you.

Dissolving Failure Beliefs to Thrive

"What we can or cannot do, what we consider possible or impossible, is rarely a function of our true capability. It is more likely a function of our beliefs about who we are."

-Anthony Robbins

A feeling of failure is enough to bring most people to a screeching halt, preventing any forward momentum. No one wants to fail. No one wants to be thought of or seen as a failure, or to feel it's paralyzing doom. Because of the magnitude of failure's intense energy in motion (as an emotion within our subconscious), we can unconsciously and radically turn to avoidance in our life just to avoid this feeling at all costs.

Getting to the root of your fears of failure and finding the underlying beliefs is key to finding joy in your own personal pursuits. We all deserve to feel significant in our own sense of self. However, failure can be a hard emotion to sense in yourself. You can often detect hidden fears of failure buried within feelings of frustration, procrastination, jealousy, resentment, and avoidance. Have you ever stopped to see how often frustration arises within you? Have you ever noticed what situations provoke procrastination? If so, you may be triggering subconscious buried fears of failure. Try addressing the beliefs listed below concerning failure to see if any of the beliefs helps you feel less frustrated and irritated with yourself and others. The good news is that the limiting beliefs below are false and are not who you are; therefore, they can be overcome.

Here are limiting beliefs you may have related to failure that could be removed. Feel free to tweak any statement that you feel needs to be addressed to make it work better for you:

Because I have failed, my family finds me unworthy.

I'm a failure if I relax.

I'm a failure if I contract an incurable disease.

I'm a failure if I am not perfect.

I'm a failure to myself if I don't work hard.

Because I am a failure, no one will love me unconditionally.

Because I have failed, I cannot love myself.

Because I fail to meet my own expectations, I feel depressed.

I create isolation in order to protect myself from my own failure.

I'm a failure because nothing ever works for me.

If I fail to meet society's expectations, I am not good enough.

When I fail, society sees me as not good enough.

If I fail the world, I have no value to my family.

If I fail the world, I have no value to God.

I'm afraid God won't find me worthy because I have failed.

Because people continue to fail me, I feel disappointed.

Because I haven't accomplished anything in my life, I'm a failure.

I'm a failure because I continue to smoke.

I'm a failure because I continue to procrastinate.

I'm a failure because I cannot lose weight.

I'm a failure because I cannot get rid of my health issue.

I'm a failure because I continue to harm myself with my addictions.

I am a failure if I cannot afford my livelihood.

I'm a failure because I continue to do the wrong things.

I'm a failure because I don't like cleaning.

I'm a failure because I can't clean my own house.

I'm a failure because I cannot communicate how I feel.

I can't express my feelings because I don't want to fail other people.

I cannot say no because I don't want to fail other people.

I'm a failure because I could not save my marriage/relationship.

I can't have too many close friends because I'm afraid to fail them.

I can't be too close to my partner because I'm afraid to fail them again.

I am a failure if I cannot meet my own expectations.

I'm a failure if I fail to look or act the part.

I'm a failure because I am not smart or talented.

I'm a failure because I cannot use my creativity.

I'm a failure because I cannot use my gifts the way I expect I should.

I'm a failure because I could not be there for my family.

I'm a failure because I can't be the mother I want to be.

I overvalue the significance of insignificant tasks so that I avoid the appearance of failure.

I tell myself that my work is boring to avoid being perceived as failing.

I have to know everything before I can get started.

If I fail at something I do, people won't take me seriously in the future.

When I have to say "no," I feel like a failure.

I had to say no, and I feel like a failure.

Motherhood/fatherhood is not for me because I'm afraid of failing as a parent.

I'm a failure because I can't take care of my own children.

I'm a failure because I can't have a child of my own.

I don't want children because I don't want to fail them as a mother/father.

Marriage is not for me because I don't want to fail another relationship.

I can't buy a house/another house because I don't want to fail at paying the mortgage.

I'm a failure because I cannot let go of the past.

I'm a failure because I cannot let go of my past mistakes.

I'm a failure if I start anything new.

I'm a failure if I start a new career.

I'm a failure because nothing works for me.

I'm a failure if people don't see me as a success.

I'm afraid to be seen as a failure.

I'm afraid to be seen as a failure concerning my addiction.

I'm afraid to be seen as a failure without my identifying career.

I'm afraid to be seen as a failure without the security of my career.

I'm a failure if I'm seen a certain way.

I'm a failure because I can't be there for people the way I would want to be.

I'm a failure because my partner doesn't view me as a perfect spouse.
I am a failure because my boss does not view me as perfect.
I'm a failure because my parents don't see me as a perfect child.
I'm a failure if I'm not perfect at everything I do.
I don't deserve a perfect life.
I don't believe perfection is possible, so I will always fail.
I'm a failure because I can never be perfect towards myself.
I'm a failure because I can never get right.
It is normal for me to feel failure about myself and my life.
It is normal for me to feel like a failure concerning my finances.
It's normal for me to feel like a failure concerning .

You can access added failure beliefs the next time you meditate. Focus on feeling and hearing the statements of failure that may have been running in your subconscious, and then pull, dissolve and cancel them out with your method of choice.

Journaling to solidify what you have learned.

Feeling unworthy and believing we have failed is a recipe for creating a life that only serves to reinforce unworthiness and a failure. After working through this chapter, what situations and events have served to reinforce unworthiness and failure beliefs for you?

_____

_____

_____

_____

_____

_____

_____

Knowing you are worthy of a great life opens up many doors. In the coming days, weeks and months record the doors that have opened for you.

_____

_____

_____

_____

_____

_____

_____

CHAPTER SEVEN

ELIMINATING FEAR AND THE NEED TO CONTROL

"Fear is only as deep as the mind allows". -Japanese Proverb

Sidelining Fear and It's Accomplices

Fear has a tendency to be the puppet master playing out in our lives interplaying in a variety of life areas from the very small to some very big fears and phobias. The places that the shadow of fear touches can play a part in where we live, the types of jobs we pursue, and the people and relationships we surround ourselves with. Fear shows up as the small voice—and then a louder voice—telling us that we cannot do something that we actually really want to do. Fear can also more covertly camouflage itself and lull us into a false sense of security, whispering that, "It is better to play it safe than to be sorry," or "security is safer than uncalculated risks." Just as a hostage can unwittingly bond with their captor, you can begin to find a familiar friend in fear. "Oh well, I did not really want to try that anyway," your subconscious can say to you. "I have a routine and this way I do things makes me feel safe.

Why change? It's much better to be familiar and comfortable." Yet the numbing effects of fearful beliefs limit you and thus prevent you from following your heart's desires.

Fear of traveling can keep you from experiencing the beauty of life, fear of not having enough money can keep you from going on vacation. Fearful thoughts can keep you from intimacy in relationships that you long for, as well as keep you from enjoying from your present moment. The shadows of fear do not always reveal their hidden agenda until a fearful moment triggers the mind. However, when that happens, life events (God perhaps) will sometimes cause a major shake up to create the realization of where that fear has limited you. Some may call it karma, or the universe wanting you to face your fears, but it is the limited perception of a situation that fear placed in your subconscious mind that created the scenario.

With this workbook, you have now been given a chance to face, dissolve and cancel beliefs related to fear. Facing a fear head on is one way to clear it, such as jumping out of a plane with a parachute if you have a fear of heights; but that is a bit more stressful than what we're recommending! Becoming aware, and then sitting with a particular fear, allows it to be brought into the light from the subconscious level then seeing it and intending for that fear to be dissipated is all that is needed to prevent that fear from manifesting on the physical level. It's also important to remember that fear usually has a few travel companions such as anxiety, panic, control, and worry. These related emotions can heighten the sense of being constantly overwhelmed.

With these interconnections in mind, below are a number of belief statements about fear, anxiety, panic, control, worry, and overwhelm that will help to free you from this false friend and its cohorts so you can start living life on your terms. If you want peace, then be willing to face your fears.

Here are limiting beliefs about fear that you can remove:

I am afraid I won't be able to cope with the unknown future.

Fear keeps me safe.

Fear is healthy.

Fear serves me.

My fear of seems normal for me.

My fear of the past sabotaging my future seems normal.

I would rather stay in fear and doubt than move forward in love.

I am afraid of having my heart broken again.

I am afraid of breaking the hearts of others.

I cannot be close to anyone out of fear of breaking their heart.

My fears and doubts are stronger than my will to change.

I get attention from my fears.

I get attention from my panic.

I get attention from being overwhelmed.

I get attention from my anxiety.

I am a slave to my fears.

I am a slave to my anxiety.

I am a slave to panic.

I live daily in fear.

I live daily fearing change.

I live daily fearing loss.

I live daily fearing success.

I live daily fearing I will make an error of forget something.

Life is overwhelming.

It is normal for me to feel overwhelmed all the time.

I am a slave to being overwhelmed.

I am afraid to let go of, and be without, fear.

People I love and God want me to be fearful.

If I let go of being in fear, I will die.

The world is full of fear.

Without my fear, my world will crumble.

I plan my life around my fear.

If I had no fear, I would be hurt by the world and the people in it.

My fears are the only reality I know thus far.

My fear is my guide.

I build my life around my fear of the past.

I will never build a life that is good enough.

I will always feel unworthy, broken and depressed.

I am doomed to a life of feeling unworthy.

I doubt I will ever feel or know that I am worthy.

I fear that if I cannot provide for my family, I will be a failure.

I fear I'm not good enough if I fail .

If I fail, I fear my life will be pointless.

If I fail my clients, then I will be unworthy.

Sacrificing for family, I fear I am still not good enough.

I fear I'm not good enough, even if I sacrifice everything.

I am afraid of failing the world.

I am afraid that my past mistakes will ruin my relationship(s) in the future.

I fear that all that I love will be taken from me.

All the progress I have made will be for nothing.

Every day, I fear the worst.

I don't know how to carry on without fear.

Everyone I love dies.

Everyone I love will meet an untimely end.

Tragedy is everywhere.

Tragedy exists around every corner.

Tragedy looms over my life.

Tragedy will strike me over and over again.

I expect tragedy.

I expect panic, fear and anxiety.

I expect to be overwhelmed.

Tragedy will take me from those that I love.

Everyone I love leaves me.

I am terrified every day.

I am terrified of life.

I am afraid all the time.

Living with fear and anxiety is normal for me.

Fear and panic are my everyday reality.

I cannot escape fear and anxiety.

My fear of life is overwhelming.

Even simple day to day tasks overwhelm me.

I cannot take on one more thing.

No one will help ease my burden.

My fear and anxiety is frustrating to others.

My panic attacks are overwhelming.

There is no hope of being free from panic, fear, and anxiety.

I am doomed to live forever in fear.

I am an anxious person.

I am a fearful person.

I am overwhelmed by panic and anxiety.

Who would I be without fear, anxiety, panic, and a sense of being overwhelmed?

I would not recognize my world without fear.

It is impossible not to be overwhelmed by life.

I am insecure and seek validation outside of myself.

My insecurities keep me stuck in negative situations.

Releasing my insecurities would be impossible.

Life has proven to me that I have reason to be insecure.

I am too insecure to speak my truth; I would be too exposed.

I feel insecure and vulnerable all the time.

I am fearful of letting go of my resistance.

It is normal for me to feel insecure and vulnerable.

I am afraid of darkness.

I am afraid of the darkness of others.

I am afraid of the light.

I have to suffer in order to face my fears.

I have to suffer in order to face my past/future fears.

I am afraid of being seen in the light.

My environment has taught me life is about living in fear.

My environment has taught me to fear what I don't understand.

I'm afraid of losing my security I worked so hard to create.

I'm afraid of losing the security in my relationship I worked so hard to create.

Here are belief affirmations to choose from to replace fearful limiting beliefs:

It is normal for me to feel safe and secure.

I release all the insecurities that kept me stuck.

I am confident in my ability to speak my truth.

It's ok to be seen in the light of God.

It's ok for others to see me in the light of God.

I trust myself to do the right thing and make the right decisions.

I have no reason to be insecure.

I move through my life with a sense of positive expectation and wonder.

I can handle every situation that comes my way with courage and confidence.

My heart and mind are filled with peace.

I shine with the light of inner peace.

I have nothing to prove.

It is safe for me to ask for help.

It is safe for me to accept help.

I am free from fear and suspicion.

It is normal for me to live free from fearful thoughts of the past/future.

It is normal for me to live free from fearful thoughts towards others.

I am free from my fear of God.

I am free from my thoughts of not being enough.

It is safe for me to ask for my needs to be met.

I am free to live my life apart from anxiety.

I am free to live my life without resistance.

My life is now different than it was when fear ruled me; it will never be the same again.

I know how to live the rest of my life free from the fear of darkness.

I can have what I want in my life free from the fear of loss.

I know how to face life free from the fear of loss.

I know how to build things in my life free from the fear of having to start over again.

I know how to have a relationship free from the fear of being forsaken by my significant other.

The fear of darkness has no power over me.

I am free from the fear of disappointing others.

I am free from the fear of disappointing myself.

I am free from the fear of disappointing the world.

I am free from suffering concerning future fears.

I am free from suffering concerning past fears.

My cells are free from the memory of fear, worry, terror.

My heart is free from the memory of fear, panic and worry.

I am free to choose new places and ideas for my future because I release all fear.

It's safe for me to release all unnecessary fears.

Releasing fear is easy for me.

I willingly release all fear of the unknown.

I am willing to receive all the positive benefits of living a life free from the fear of the unknown.

Possible beliefs to clear concerning past and future fears:

I fear more grief and loss is in my future.

I am fearful that my past mistakes will destroy my future.

I am fearful that I won't be good enough in the future.

I am fearful that I won't be able to afford my life financially in the future.

I am fearful my relationship won't be the same in the future as it is today.

Fear of my past is normal for me.

Fear of my future is normal for me.

I am terrified of losing future money in the stock market.

I am fearful of being alone in the future.

I am afraid of dying alone in the future.

I am afraid of a loved one dying soon in the future.

I am fearful of losing control over my future.

I'm fearful of experiencing abusive situations in the future.

I'm terrified of experiencing betrayal in the future.

I'm fearful of experiencing betrayal in a future relationship.

I am anxious about losing control over my relationship in the future.

I would rather stay in doubt concerning the future of my relationship than move forward in love.

I fear the guilt I will feel should my past catch up with me.

I am afraid my past mistakes will ruin my relationship in the future.

I fear the rejection I would feel should my past catch up to me.

I fear the abandonment I would feel should my past catch up with me.

I expect loss and tragedy in the future.

I am afraid I will continue to be sick, even in the future.

I am fearful of being abandoned by those I love in the future.

I am afraid I will be punished in the future because of my past.

I am afraid I will be rejected in the future because of my past.

I am fearful of experiencing continual unworthiness in future.

I am fearful of the change that will come in the unknown future.

I am fearful of changing my job/career in the future.

I am terrified of having another child in the future.

I am terrified of experiencing a disease in the future.

I am terrified of aging/getting older in the future.

I am afraid of not having any control over my future.

I am afraid of being seen as a disappointment in the future.

You can select from among these belief affirmations to replace past and future fears:

I know how to be in harmony with my future.

I know how to be in harmony with my future relationships.

I know how to be in harmony with my future concerning money and security.

It is normal for me to be in harmony concerning my past.

I know how to live free from fear concerning the past.

I know how to live my day-to-day life free from frustration in my heart concerning the past.

I know how to live my future life free from feeling abandoned.

I know how to live my future life free from betrayal.

I know how to live my future life free from rejection.

I know how to live my future life free from insecurity and loss.

I know how to live my future life feeling free from the past.

I know how to live my future life feeling supported by life, God, and the universe.

I am confident about taking positive steps towards the future I desire for me.

I allow all fears concerning the past to dissolve completely.

I allow myself to experience the future I have dreamed of.

I welcome a future filled with abundance of love, joy, peace and wealth.

My future is bright.

I am a magnet for wonderful things.

Belief Work in Action

Beliefs cleared:

I'm afraid to be exposed.

I'm afraid that if I speak my truth, I'll feel vulnerable and exposed.

I'm afraid that if I speak my truth, I'll be hurt or judged.

I'm insecure in this world.

It is abnormal for me to express my voice.

Several fear beliefs came up for a client Cecelia, who mostly came to see Mayline for chronic neck pain and multiple allergy issues. Cecilia also dealt with a myriad of thyroid issues, anxiety and panic attacks combined with severe depression that had plagued her life.

Muscle testing the chakras of her throat and heart and then doing clearing work on certain specific emotions, helped initially. But after several energy healing sessions, a few areas were continually being blocked. Mayline knew there had to be more subconscious beliefs still creating emotional triggers for her. So she muscle tested and uncovered, "I am afraid to speak my truth, I will feel vulnerable and exposed." Mayline then tapped in, "I can speak my truth free from fear or judgement from others." Initially Cecilia's arm, which was being used as a biofeedback tool, weakened, indicating that her subconscious did not believe that positive belief statement. Mayline then tested Cecilia for the other fear beliefs listed above. All the limiting beliefs muscle tested firmly, meaning she believed them strongly, and therefore, they needed to be cleared. Her subconscious believed these negative statements to be true. Cecelia agreed and stated that, "yes," she had indeed struggled to speak her own truth in past situations.

Using the Manual Prayer Method from Chapter three and the phrase "Pull, dissolve and cancel," Mayline asked Spirit to pull, dissolve and cancel the multiple fear beliefs one at a time. Immediately, a huge rush of energy shifted for Cecelia that both of them felt. As a fairly intuitive person, Cecelia, after clearing all the beliefs, felt she had run a marathon and reported a strange tingling sensation going on in the area of her kidneys (in Chinese Medicine, the kidneys are associated with fears, anxieties, and panic). Tapping in and replacing the affirmations of "I am allowed to live in this world free from insecurities," and "It's safe for me to speak my truth free judgment and fear of being hurt," Mayline made sure that the subconscious was reprogrammed correctly confirming the new beliefs held strong.

Some additional fear beliefs to consider removing include:

I'm afraid of intimacy.
I'm afraid of hurting others.
I am afraid of being lied to.
I'm afraid people will forsake me if they knew of my past.
Because of my failures, I'm afraid people will forsake me.
Because of my past failures, people will forsake me in the future.
I'm afraid I'll never get well.
I'm afraid to change.
I'm afraid of change and what it might bring.
I'm afraid of places I am not familiar with.
I'm afraid I won't find peace in my life.
I'm afraid I won't be loved.
I am suspicious that what I have won't last.
I am suspicious of opportunities that come too easy.
I am suspicious of people that are too nice.
I am suspicious of religious people.
I am suspicious of people of a certain race.
I am suspicious of the motives of others.
Other people are suspicious of me.
I am suspicious of what others think of me.
I am suspicious of people getting close to me.
I am suspicious of how people will think of my past.
Suspicion rules my world.
Suspicion rules my actions.
I am suspicious that my relationship won't last.
I am suspicious of the medical community.
I am suspicious that if I get married, my relationship won't last.
It is normal for me to stay suspicious.
I am fearful that what I have now will not last.
I am afraid I will be embarrassed.
I am afraid I will lose what I know, and my life will be different.
I am afraid it is not the right time for me to move on.
I am afraid I will be punished.
I am afraid I will be disappointed.

I'm afraid I won't be satisfied.

I'm afraid I'll be abandoned.

I'm afraid I'll be rejected.

I'm afraid I'll be deceived.

I'm afraid I'll be left behind.

I'm afraid of disease.

I am afraid of germs.

I am afraid I will become diseased.

I am afraid I will become sick.

I am afraid people I love will become sick.

I'm afraid I'll be exposed.

I'm afraid I will be punished if I am exposed.

My fear is serving me.

I have no patience for people who want to live in fear.

I would rather stay in my fear of than to move forward in love.

My fear is protecting me from disappointment.

My fear protects me from certain people.

My fear protects me from making mistakes.

My fear protects me from getting hurt.

My fear allows me to keep people away.

Fear should control me.

Without fear, I would fail.

I allow fear to control me.

I must fear God.

I must have fear in my life concerning .

I must have fear in my life concerning the past and past mistakes.

I have an agreement/contract with fear.

I fear freedom and happiness.

I fear success and wealth.

I fear love.

I fear that it is too late for me to do something new.

I fear that I have missed too many opportunities to be successful.

The world cannot exist without fear.

Fear runs my life.

Healing is not safe.

Love is not safe.

Healthy relationships are not safe for me.
Sex is not safe.
Being alone is not safe.
Money is not safe.
Being happy is not safe.
Life is not safe.
I am not safe at the .
I am not safe at work.
Tragedy will happen at work.
Tragedy will happen in my home.
Tragedy will happen in public spaces.
It is not safe to be in public.
It is not safe to be noticed.
It is only safe to be invisible to others.
If I do nothing, then I will be safe.
If I accomplish my goals, I will not be safe.
If I accomplish my goals, I will still be disappointed.
If I accomplish my goals, tragedy will take it all away.
If I have a great and happy life, it will all be taken from me.
I can never be happy because if I am, I will lose everything.
I am not safe at home.
I am not safe outside.
I am not safe in public spaces.
I will not be safe if I clear my beliefs about fear.
No one I love is safe.
Safety does not really exist.
Nothing is safe.
No one is safe.
I can never be safe.
It is normal for me to feel unsafe.
No one I love will ever be safe.
People who don't look, think, or act like me are not safe.
Letting go of my fears is not safe.
People will always fear and hate.
Letting go of my old patterns and beliefs is not safe.
If I go on vacation, terrible things will happen.

If I accept new opportunities, terrible things will happen.
If I move on, terrible things will happen.
If I try something new, bad things will happen.
I'm afraid the worst is going to happen.
I always have to prepare for the worst.
I'm afraid there is something terribly wrong with me.
I'm afraid of dying from disease.
I'm afraid I'll die early.
I'm afraid I'll never be accepted.
I'm afraid I'll never be accomplished or successful.
I am afraid I will be accomplished and successful.
I am afraid of being accomplished and successful.
I'm afraid I'll fail my family.
I'm afraid I'll fail God.
I'm afraid I'll fail myself.
I'm afraid my spouse won't find me attractive.
I am afraid to be attractive.
It is not safe to be attractive.
I am afraid of unwanted attention.
I am afraid of compliments as they make me uncomfortable.
I'm afraid I'll lose my spouse.
I'm afraid the world will find me unworthy.
I'm afraid I'm not worthy.
I'm afraid people will mock me.
I'm afraid of my life mission.
I'm afraid I'll lose myself.
I'm afraid I'll never get ahead in life.
I'm afraid I'll never get better.
I'm afraid I'll get a disease.
I'm afraid I'll die an early death.
It benefits me to live in fear.
I'm afraid of good things.
I'm afraid of people.
I'm afraid of the world, so I can't act in it.
I'm afraid of being hurt.
I am too afraid to fail, so I will not even begin.

I'm afraid of becoming like my mother.

I'm afraid of becoming like my father.

I am afraid of doing this work and connecting more to my higher self and to God.

I am afraid all the time; it is the only way I know how to live.

I'm afraid of being seen as a disappointment by my parents.

I'm afraid of being seen as a disappointment by the world.

I am afraid of being seen as a disappointment by myself.

I am afraid of being seen as a disappointment by my spouse.

I afraid of being seen as a disappointment.

I am afraid of being seen as a disappointment by society.

I worry I won't amount to much and thereby be a disappointment.

I worry I will end up a disappointment.

I am afraid I will be a disappointment to God.

At any moment, I could lose everything.

I am vulnerable and exposed.

I am so scared.

I am too scared to let go of my limiting beliefs.

It is not safe for me to be unlimited in my beliefs.

It is not safe for me to move on from any of the following: pain, suffering, guilt, blame, shame, and hate.

It is not safe for me to follow my dreams.

It is not safe for me to heal.

It is not safe for me to forgive myself or others.

I am never safe.

Here are a few more belief affirmations for dissolving fear:

I am no longer afraid.

I am willing to receive all the benefits of living a life free from suspicion.

I move forward in my life free from fear that used to hold me in place.

I can allow myself to live my life without fear and suspicion.

I willingly hand over my fears to God and accept all his help in my life.

It is normal for me to feel courageous.

It is possible to live a life free from suspicion.

It is safe for me to live free from suspicion of people.

I am safe to move on with my plans.

It is normal for me to feel safe wherever I go.

It is healthy for me to be conscious of my surroundings to keep me safe, but I no longer have to be a victim of my own fear.

I believe that I am healed from the burden of too much fear.

Fear no longer guides my decisions.

Fear no longer chooses for me.

Even though I feel fear at times, it does not rule my life.

I can live my life now knowing that I have all that I need within me to overcome fear whenever it comes up.

I have conquered fear.

Love lights the darkness where fear once haunted.

Loosening Up The Reigns of Control

"You may not control all the events that happen to you, but you can decide not to be reduced by them." -Maya Angelou

To be or not to be? To have control or to not have control? That is the question. Do we actually have any control over our lives? Or is life one big roller coaster?

Control comes in many forms and many names: ego, discipline, restraint, constraint, or curbing, limiting and regulating. We grow up hearing, "Take control over your life!" or "If you don't control yourself, you're going to get into trouble and not amount to anything." Our need for external controls affect us and those forms of control can be as big as societal rules and norms we are expected to meet, or family expectations. Too much control doesn't allow much spontaneity. Controlling energy can be like a vice grip over life. It is the uptight boss who has to appear to have control over everything and every situation, or the overly restrictive mother wanting to control her only child. On

113

the opposite end of the spectrum is a young person who refuses to take on any responsibilities, and so their life spirals out of control. In reality we are like a captain of a ship, making our way through alternating smooth and calm waters.

A balance then is desired of knowing when to let go of certain ideas, processes and things, and when to take control. Because control squelches energy in many areas of life. We have listed limiting beliefs that focus on control as a form of fear. Others encompass control beliefs that would cause internal conflict and limit your life from expanding fully. In their place, you will want to tap in beliefs that support the process of surrendering control to God/Higher Self.You may also want to consider adding affirmations that bring in structure if you feel your life is too spread out and you are reeling out of control on some level. After all, life is a balancing act and you are ultimately the best judge of what areas of your life require more letting of control or structure.

When you do surrender your own personal grips of control to God/ Higher Self, your ability to create the life you want can expand with far more ease and flow.

Here are limiting beliefs surrounding control as a form of fear that you may want to clear:

I must be in control at all times in order to feel safe.
New situations are not safe.
I must control my future.
I must control the unknown future.
If I do not control my future, life will be unsafe.
If I do not control my money, life will be unsafe.
If I do not control my health, life will be unsafe.
If I do not control my energy expenditure, I will be exhausted.

I am not in control of anything, and that is unsafe.

I'm afraid of losing control over my health.

I must be in control of my relationships.

I must be in control of my security that I worked so hard to create.

I am afraid of losing control of my relationships.

If I'm not careful someone will kill me because I live in a hostile world.

Because I cannot control others, going into public spaces is unsafe.

I'm afraid to lose control over my finances.

I believe she/he will leave me and I need to try to control them in order to prevent that.

I'm afraid of losing control over my space.

I'm afraid if my beliefs are being perceived wrongly by others, I'll be harmed.

Because I have been a victim, I have no control.

I have to be in control of my emotions.

I must control my emotions or else I'll feel/be vulnerable.

I'm afraid of losing control over my emotions.

I hate to be exposed.

If I don't control my emotions, I'll appear foolish/silly/outspoken/out of line, or I'll be seen as childish.

I have to be in control of any project in order to ensure that it is done right.

If you want something done right, you have to do it yourself.

I have to do everything myself or it will just create more work that I have to do.

I must be in charge or else I will appear weak.

I have to be control of my self-image.

If I'm not in control of my emotions, I'll be too vulnerable.

I must control my time.

I am expected to do everything myself, so I have to control as much as possible.

Others control my life/destiny.

I have no control over anything.

I feel out of control all the time.

I have to give control of my life over to others in order to be loved.

I must control my time or else I'll be late.

I must control my money so a man/woman doesn't take it from me.

I must control my self-image.

I must control how I'm being perceived by others.

I must control my environment.

I must control how much money I spend/make.

I'm afraid of losing control of how people see me

I must control the self-image I project.

I must control the image of what others perceive me to be.

I won't allow a man take care of me because I don't forgive them.

I won't allow a man to control me because it will only end in disappointment.

I have to control my diet or else I'll be fat.

I have to control my internal state.

I have to control my sleeping patterns in order to function.

I have to control my energy expenditure.

I have to control my anger towards other people.

I have to control my vengefulness towards other people.

Pushing myself helps me to feel in control.

Having things in place allows me to relax and be in control.

Focusing on goals allows me to stay in control.

Cleaning makes me feel in control.

Having my environment be in perfect order makes me feel in control.

Being right makes me feel in control.

I have to be right in order to feel in control.

To be wrong is to feel out of control.

I have to control my energy output so I am not tired

People who don't control their lives are not respectable.

I must control my future.

I have to control where I spend my time.

I have to control my time and those I spend time with.

My time is limited.

I hate that I spend all my time working.

I hate that I feel controlled by my family.

I hate that I feel controlled by my partner.

I fear those who want to control me.

I hate a partner/spouse that threatens to control me.

My circumstances have complete control over my time.

Time to myself is impossible to control.

I have no time to do anything.

My time is limited, and I must control my time.

If I'm not in control, then I won't know how to act.

If I control my diet, then I won't get fat.

If I control how much I eat, then it won't affect my digestion.

If I control how much I eat, I won't feel so badly.

Being in control means I'm strong.

I worry that I won't be able to control my future.

I have to control my partner and friends, or they will leave me.

People who feel free to live as they want make me angry and uncomfortable.

Nothing happens unless I want it to.

It's dangerous to be out of control.

Limiting beliefs that lead you to feel out of control:

I have no control over my life.

I don't want to be in control of my own life; it is too much responsibility.

If I take control of my own life, I will fail.

I'm too young to control my life.

I hate people that want to control me.

Its normal for me to feel out of control.

It's normal for me to feel emotionally out of control.

I have lived my entire life under the thumb of controlling people; I don't know any other way.

To make a mistake is to feel out of control.

If internal things aren't in place the way I want, then I feel out of control.

If external things aren't in place the way I want, I feel out of control.

You can tap in some of these belief affirmations to replace limiting beliefs on control:

I live in a friendly world.

I allow only positive energies to flow into my life.

I know when to let go and how to let go.

I can allow others to take responsibility for their own lives.

I can allow myself to accept responsibility for my life.

I have no need to control others.

I can feel in control without having everything be in perfect order around me.

I release all desire to control others.

I release all desire to control outcomes, and trust God in the handling of all my affairs.

I am willing to receive all the positive benefits of letting go of excessive control over my life.

I give myself permission to release all forms of control from my life.

It is safe for me to let go of control and learn to trust.

My soul knows what it feels like to live a life free from control.

I give closure to all past control, for it has no power over my life today.

I live in the present and design my future.

I release the need to be right all the time.

I let go of old, outdated thoughts and ideas that prevent me from living my true purpose.

I accept myself for what I am, and I better myself everyday.

I am assertive in my life, and I pursue my goals and dreams.

I give myself permission to be at one with the universe around me.

I am more than my fears.

I am deserving of a life free to follow my dreams.

I am in control of my own life fear is not.

I release the need to have fear control my life.

My dreams and goals will come to pass without me having to control all the variables.

I can allow others to express their ideas and opinions without needing to talk over them.

I can accept that other people might have good ideas.

I no longer need to be in control of everything.

I no longer need to be controlled by others.

I trust that I can make my own decisions and build my life the way that makes me happy.

It is normal for me to live free from control and move into creativity.

I have control over fear and over my own reactions.

There is so much good in the world.

It is normal for me to be creative vs controlling.

There is so much love and peace in the world.

I experience the world as a beautiful place filled with joy.

I can see all the love and light in the world.

I forgive myself for previously allowing fear and control to guide me.

Journaling to solidify what you have learned

In what ways has fear played a part in the decisions you have made in your life? What fears are you working through?

_____

_____

_____

_____

_____

_____

_____

In what areas of your life have you tried to be in control but that control energy actually became a hindrance?

_____

_____

_____

_____

_____

_____

_____

Did you experience moments of resistance while working through these limiting beliefs related to control? If so, how were you able to move past those moments?

_____

_____

_____

_____

_____

_____

_____

CHAPTER EIGHT

CLEARING OUT THE COUSINS OF FEAR: WORRY AND DOUBT

Worry often gives a small thing a big shadow.
-Swedish Proverb

Freeing Yourself from Worry

Unfortunately, fear has a few cousins, one of which is worry. Where fear tends to sit energetically in the kidneys, worry will tend to sit energetically in the spleen and heart (according to Chinese Medicine). Too much worry will literally make you sick by weakening the spleen and lowering your body's immune system. Worry about what hasn't yet happened, or how past circumstances could thwart unknown future events, is completely useless. Yet we all have wasted much of our time in service of worry. In order to truly let go of fear as a factor in your life, you have to wade through the muck and clear out its cousin, worry, as well.

Here are limiting beliefs you can clear related to worry:

I am worried all the time.

Everybody worries.

A good parent worries about their children and the future.

I don't know how to live without worry.

I am a slave to worry.

Worry is normal and not a big deal.

Everyone worries; why should I be any different?

I worry about my family having enough and being safe.

I worry I won't have enough or be safe.

I worry when there's nothing to worry about.

I worry about my kids and the choices they make and if they are safe.

I worry that I will fail.

I worry that I will succeed, and that my life might look different.

I worry about money.

I worry about time.

I worry about work and home.

I worry about responsibility.

I worry about retirement.

I worry about what people think of me, or will think of me.

I worry that my family worries about me.

I worry I have too much to do.

I worry the timing is all wrong.

I worry that I am too late.

I worry I will not be able to handle my dreams coming true.

I worry I won't live up to my potential.

Worry is part of who I am.

God wants me to worry.

I worry because no one else will.

I'm worried that I am the only one who is responsible.

Someone has to worry about things.

I worry I am not doing a good job at .

I worry that my boss thinks I am not doing good enough.

I worry my coworkers think I am not doing good enough.

I worry my classmates think badly of me.

I worry about bills.

Worry is helpful.

Worry keeps me in check.

It is safe to worry all the time.

Without worry, I would not be prepared if bad things happen.

I worry bad things will happen to me and the people I love.

I worry I am too weak.

I worry I will never feel good again.

I worry I am too broken to ever be happy again.

I worry I will never get through .

I worry my relationships will fall apart.

I worry about what people think of me.

I worry about fitting in and being accepted.

I worry that I am not prepared enough.

I worry that others will drop the ball, and I will have to pick up the slack.

I worry others are not committed enough.

I worry that I will always have to do everything myself.

I worry about placing trust in others.

I worry about making wrong decisions.

I worry about hurting the feelings of others to the point that I sacrifice my happiness.

I worry that I will get hurt.

I worry about things I cannot control.

I worry about my health and the health of the people I love.

I worry no one loves me or will love me.

I worry that my family does not know how much I really love them.

I worry that sharing how I feel with others will backfire and I will be hurt.

I worry that I will be rejected by people in my life if I achieve my goals.

I am worried that if I do too much, people will take advantage of me.

It is necessary to worry in order to live.

I don't know how to live without worry.

I don't know who I am without worry.

It is not possible for me to live without worry.

Freedom from my worries is not attainable.

I worry that I am stuck where I am.

I worry myself sick.

I worry I won't know what to say or do.

I worry I will say or do the wrong thing.

Belief affirmations you can tap in to fill the previous space of worry include:

I know how to live free from worry.

I deeply love and accept myself even though I do worry.

I know what it feels like to explore all the areas of an idea without getting stuck in worry.

I am free from the limits that worry placed on me.

I accept a life free from worry.

I am worthy of being free from worry.

God knows that I am worthy of being free from worry.

I know who I am without worry.

It is safe for me to be free from worry.

I can face the future consequences without worry.

I can allow my life to be free from worry.

I can forgive myself for believing that I have to be worried in life.

I give myself permission to let go of living with daily worry.

It is normal for me to be free from worrying.

It is normal for me to be free from doubt.

I move forward in my life with strength and confidence.

I am able to place trust in myself.

I am able to place trust in others.

I am able to place trust in God.

Addressing Inevitable Moments of Doubt

"Our doubts are traitors and make us lose the good we oft might win by fearing to attempt."

Shakespeare

Up until this point, it may have been impossible for you to go through life without doubt. The emotion of doubt is the energy we confront on the way to feeling certainty and stronger faith in ourselves. In one sense, you can be thankful for a path that includes doubt. In fact, because of doubt, we will try out approaches that help us to gain confidence in them and build a certain faith in ourselves as a result.

Doubt nonetheless can be a cobweb that keeps you from realizing your fullest potential in anything, and it can hinder the process of completing things as well as make you distrust past progress. You know you want to step up but there is hesitation in your step, a looking over the shoulder of, "Am I really doing the right thing?" Yet when you pull out the layers of doubt in your subconscious, the days can become brighter and your ability to step forward is stronger, as you confidently look forward to the future without questioning anything. Recognizing the doubt that affects how you are perceiving certain situations and clearing any negative beliefs surrounding particular issues will help to move you past challenges.

Some limiting beliefs to consider clearing concerning doubt include:

I doubt I am on my right path.

I doubt my ability to function on my own.

I doubt my ability to function on my own without being codependent on a man/woman.

Because I doubt my own goodness, I am not worthy of God's love.

Because I doubt my own goodness, I am not confident around other people.

Because I doubt my own goodness, I need to punish myself.

Because I doubt my own goodness, God cannot love me.

I live daily with doubt.

I doubt I am good enough for anyone to love.

Because I doubt my own willpower, I cannot give up my addiction.

I doubt I have any power.

I doubt my own willpower to follow through on any project because I will fail anyway.

Because I doubt my own intelligence, I cannot succeed at anything I try.

Because I doubt my own goodness It's impossible for me to enjoy life fully.

Because I doubt my own abilities, it's impossible to be successful in/at .

I doubt my own ability to stay connected to my Higher Self; therefore, I cannot be successful in/at .

Because I doubt my own goodness, I must stay guilty of my past mistakes.

I can't escape my past because of my own self doubt.

I cannot be present in the moment because of my self-doubt.

I can't escape my past because I was abused and that causes me doubt.

I can't escape my past because of my religious upbringing, and I doubt who I am.

I cannot live in the moment because of my self doubt.

I can't live in the moment because I can't escape my past.

I can't live in the moment because I can't deal with my feelings of self doubt.

I doubt my ability to live a life free from my addiction.

I doubt my ability to feel worthy of God.

I doubt my ability to feel worthy of a healthy relationship.

I doubt my ability to feel worthy of a purposeful life.

I doubt my own ability to say "no."

I doubt my ability to stay in the present moment because people invade my space.

I doubt my ability to stay in the present moment because I am afraid of my own thoughts.

I doubt my ability to speak my truth.

I doubt my ability to listen to my own intuition.

I doubt my ability to trust the answers in front of me.

I doubt my ability to make a decision and be comfortable with it.

I doubt my ability to trust my decisions.

Feeling worthy is impossible because I doubt my future success.

Feeling worthy is impossible because I doubt where I should even start.

I need to doubt myself in order to live.

I need to doubt others in order to protect myself.

I doubt my ability to love myself completely.

I doubt my ability to feel worthy about myself the way that I am.

I doubt my ability to feel worthy about myself because I have failed so many times in the past.

I doubt my ability to accept myself the way I am.

I doubt my ability to accept my body the way it is.

I doubt my ability to accept my relationship the way it is.

I doubt my ability to accept people as they are.

I doubt my ability to be flexible with people.

Belief affirmations that you can use to replace doubt beliefs with include:

Faith is deserving of my trust.

I can put my trust in my own abilities.

I can put my trust in faith.

Without trust, I can't form a meaningful relationship with anyone.

I can accept who I am without doubt.

I know how it feels to live my day-to-day life believing in myself.

I accept that my life is free of all self-doubt.

I'm allowed feelings of confidence.

I know how to live with believing completely that my life will work out just fine.

I am free from doubt now and forever.

I give myself permission to be free from doubt.

There is no room for doubt in my life.

My cells are free from the memory of doubt.

My heart is free from the memory of self-doubt.

All of my doubts have been replaced with faith and love.

I release the need to have doubts that I am worthy.

I release all beliefs that I cannot be free from doubts.

It is safe for me to be my true self without doubt.

I forgive myself for having doubted God.

I forgive myself for doubting my own worth.

I forgive others who have doubted me.

I am free now to trust in myself and others.

I am free now to trust that life will work out for the better.

I know how to trust my future without doubt.

It is normal for me to know that I a free of doubt.

Even though I doubt, I love and accept myself unconditionally.

CHAPTER NINE

ELIMINATING GUILT, BLAME, AND SHAME

"If one is still blaming another for the injury of the heart, he has not yet healed the heart." -Paul Selig

Shame is a weighted emotion that tends to control human behavior. Despite the shame, guilt or blame we feel about ourselves, it is what you believe about yourself that is true. When we feel shame, guilt, or blame, we build walls around ourselves that block out higher more loving frequencies. It's the lower frequencies of emotions constructed into beliefs that keep others at a distance and sabotage new opportunities from happening. The undeserving beliefs you hold prevent you from accepting good things in your life. Beliefs related to guilt, shame and blame can especially run deep and lead to emotional toxicity and energetic stagnation. Blame is different from shame and is an emotionally spiked form of condemnation of someone who we think has wronged us in some manner.

When your blame is directed at someone else then it only limits you and not the other person. Meaning, that if someone has harmed you in some way, it is far better that you shift energetically away from blame.

Your pain is not necessarily their fault but perhaps an area of letting go of certain limiting beliefs around a situation. Having an awareness of this type of process will help to heal the reason you are triggered or "blaming" someone in the first place. If we can heal ourselves and our feelings towards those who have wronged us, moving forward through life would feel more peaceful. Blame is never about someone else, it is always about you and the deep seated hurt that is being triggered inside that needs to surface in order to be healed.

Here are a number of beliefs to clear on Guilt, Blame, and Shame.

Limiting Beliefs on Guilt:

I was born to be taken advantage of because I am guilty.

I was born to be depressed because I am guilty.

I was born to lose because I am guilty.

Feeling guilty makes things right for my past.

If I say something wrong I must feel guilty.

If I'm not a certain weight I feel guilty.

Feeling guilty makes me feel better.

I must punish myself with guilt for not meeting my own expectations.

My guilt will cause me to fail future expectations.

I must punish myself with guilt for not meeting my partners expectations.

Because I am guilty I must give to the point of exhaustion.

I am not worthy unless I work to the point of exhaustion.

Because I am guilty I must work to the point of exhaustion.

To appease my guilt, I must give until I have nothing left in order to prove myself to God.

Everyone else must come before me.

It is not possible to put myself first.

My children must come first.

I feel guilty if I don't put my children first.

Serving others must come first.

My (insert your relationship) must come first.

I feel guilty if I don't place my relationship first.

I deserve a life of hardship and toil because I am guilty.

I am not capable of letting go of my guilt.

My personal drama keeps the world from seeing my failure.

I measure my weakness against other strengths.

I feel guilty when there's no one else for me to help.

I feel guilty when I am doing something for myself.

I feel guilty when I have to spend money on myself.

I feel guilty when I have to disappoint someone.

Guilt controls me.

I wear my guilt like a badge.

I try to distract myself from my guilt with my addiction.

I must keep my ego in check or I will feel guilty.

Guilt will not let me take back my power.

My religion has taught me I am guilty of sin.

I have so much guilt it is impossible to love myself.

I have so much guilt it is impossible to forgive myself completely.

I am a slave to my guilt.

I am guilty of wanting more than I have.

I feel guilty of wanting more than my parents had.

If I have a better life I will feel guilty.

If I have make more money than my spouse I will feel guilty.

If good things happen to me I feel guilty.

If I get the things I want I feel guilty.

Spending money causes me uncontrollable guilt.

Because I have hurt others, I must feel guilty for the rest of my life.

Because I have hurt God, I must feel guilty for the rest of my life.

I am comfortable with my guilt.

Guilt has become part of me.

Guilt consumes me no matter what I do.

I can never do enough good in the world to make me free from guilt.

The weight of guilt will always be with me.

Guilt is all the is and all there will ever be for me.

I want and deserve to feel guilty.

I use guilt as a weapon against God, myself and others.

If I feel guilty then no one can tell me I am not doing my part.

Guilt is an old friend, letting it go is too much for me.

If I do anything nice for myself I feel guilty.

I can't allow anyone to do anything nice for me because of my guilt.

If I love myself and treat myself with respect I will feel guilty.

If I make a better life for myself it will hurt the people I love.

If I make a better life for myself I will feel too guilty.

It is easier to feel guilty.

It is normal for me to feel guilty.

The guilt I feel is exactly what people want for me.

Everyone thinks I am guilty.

My guilt is the only thing the world sees in me.

God thinks I am guilty.

My guilt is the only thing everyone sees about me.

I feel guilty for not making enough money.

I feel guilty if I have a lot of money.

I feel guilty/shameful for wanting a lot of money.

I feel guilty if I'm not working enough.

I don't know how to live my life without self recrimination of my past mistakes.

It's impossible to live without self recriminating thoughts concerning my past mistakes.

Limiting Beliefs on Blame:

It's easier to blame others than taking responsibility.

I blame the world for where I'm at.

If my plans don't work out the way I want I blame someone else.

I will always be held captive by my guilt, shame and blame.

I blame myself for things never going right.

I blame myself for my past relationships falling apart.

I blame myself for not taking responsibility like I should.

I blame others to prevent me from feeling guilty.

Blame is easy to hold on to.

Blame is important so I don't look bad.

God blames me.

I blame myself for not doing better.

It's normal to blame others.

It is easy to blame others.

I live daily in the past blaming what has happened on others/myself.

It is easy to find fault with other people.

It is easy to find fault with myself.

My family blames me.

My friends blame me.

My coworkers blame me.

My (spouse) blames me.

It is everyone else's fault.

It's God's fault.

It is my ego's fault.

It's my fault every time something goes wrong.

Because I am not perfect it is my fault things do not work out.

I want to blame myself or others.

I have to put the blame on others to keep from seeing what is my fault.

I blame myself before anyone else can.

I am terrified to be blamed in the future.

I must accept blame as it is expected of me.

It is honorable to accept all the blame.

It is my duty to accept all of the blame.

It is my lot in life to be blamed for everything.

I am never good enough to escape being blamed.

I have made too many mistakes not to be blamed.

God wants me to blame or find fault with others.

Everyone blames me.

When something goes wrong, it's all my fault.

Blaming others gives me something to talk about.

It's easier to blame others rather than taking responsibility.

Someone is always to blame, it may as well be me.

I feel justified and superior when I blame others.

Letting go of blame is foolish and impossible.

Finding fault with others gives me something to complain about.

I am a slave to my addiction of self blame, self shaming, and feeling guilty.

I am not capable of letting go of blame.

I can't do anything right.

I find fault with the world in order to improve it.

I find fault with myself in order to improve me.

It's my parents fault for .

Is easy for me to find fault in my relationship in order to improve it.

I mess up all the time.

I will always be blamed.

My won't let me become who I want to be.

It is my fault if I am there or if I am not.

I make poor choices and bad decisions.

I am a bad person.

I am a bad kid.

I am a bad employee.

I am a bad .

Everything will always turn out bad because it is my fault.

I feel like I am always messing up.

I feel like I am always wrong.

I feel like I am always in trouble.

I hurt everyone I love by being me.

I always do the wrong thing.

I make matters worse.

I make a mess of things.

I have failed as a (insert your relationship). Example: mother, Father, Son, daughter, spouse .

I am the cause of everyone's problems.

I am the root of everyone's problems.

I ruin everything.

Everyone is always blaming me.

I cause everything to go wrong.

I deserve to be in trouble all of the time.

Everything I do fails and therefore is my fault.

I will be at fault to God if I am exposed.

I have failed as a friend, therefore I am to blame.

I have failed God, therefore I am to blame.

I have failed myself, therefore others are to blame.

I have failed as a (insert your relationship). Example: mother, Father, Son, daughter, spouse.

Everyone is always mad at me.

If I fault, then I am of no value.

If I am at fault, then I am no value to God.

Limiting beliefs on Shame:

Society will shame me for putting myself first.

God will shame me for putting myself first.

My family and friends will turn against me if I see to my own needs first.

Putting myself first is a sin.

I do not deserve to put myself first because I am ashamed.

Spending money and time on myself is shameful.

Putting my own needs first is shameful.

I am ashamed of my own success.

I am ashamed of not being financially stable.

I am ashamed of having a healthy relationship when others are struggling.

My family is ashamed of me.

God is ashamed of me.

I am ashamed my dreams and goals are not what my parents or society expects from me.

I am ashamed for letting people I love down.

My (enter your relationship) is ashamed of me.

My friends are ashamed of me.

I am ashamed of loving myself.

I am not capable of letting go of my shame.

I do not deserve to love myself enough.

It is selfish for me to want to be free from blame, shame and guilt

I do not deserve to have an easy path.

I do not deserve help, my shame is too great.

Staying a victim shields me from seeing my own failure.

I am ashamed of ever having been a victim.

I am ashamed of my emotions.

I am ashamed of my reactions to others.

I loathe my shameful past.

I'm terrified of my future judgment and shame.

I loathe my shameful addictions.

I loathe myself for feeling shameful.

I am shameful of my desire to loathe people.

I am shameful of my desire to loathe people that seem better than me.

I loathe others for making me feel ashamed.

I loath others for making do things I am ashamed of.

Because I have done things to be ashamed of, it is right for me to loathe myself.

My shame is loathsome.

My family loathes me.

Because of my shame others loathe me.

God loathes me because I have done things to be ashamed of.

The emotions of blame, shame and guilt are not easy to feel as they can all be very deeply felt and can cut to the core. What is provided here is a great start to help heal the parts of yourself that have been buried by subconscious feelings of shame and blame and guilt. Healing all aspects of these emotions allows you to embark on the rest of your life feeling more serenity about yourself. You have the tools to no longer be chained to these beliefs. Tap in the positive beliefs and you will begin to feel better.

Recommended belief affirmations to replace the limiting beliefs just cleared:

I am honest and comfortable with who I am, and who I am becoming.

I take responsibility for who I am and who I am becoming.

It is safe to let go of blame.

Letting go of blame does not mean that I condone bad behavior.

I give myself permission to let go of all blame: past, present and future.

I choose to recognize and learn beneficially from all my experiences rather than blame.

I am respecting and supporting myself daily.

The only person I am truly responsible for is me.

I love myself enough to not use escapism as an outlet.

I love myself enough to quit any addiction.

I have nothing to prove in life; I am free to do what bring me joy and happiness.

I know how to live my life without self recriminating thoughts.

I can choose a life free from self-recrimination.

I can love myself unconditionally despite my past mistakes.

I know how to live my life free from guilt.

I give myself permission to be free from guilt.

I deserve to be free from guilt.

I am free from all future judgment and shame.

I deserve a life free from self-loathing.

Because I am free from guilt and can forgive others easily.

I know how to live my day to day life free from guilt, blame and shame.

I am a valuable and worthy person even though I have made mistakes.

I am able to move past my blame of others in order to heal.

I have the power to live my life free from guilt.

I forgive myself for having lived from a place guilt/shame/blame.

I completely accept myself.

I am able to forgive.

My soul is allowed to receive love free from shame.

My soul is allowed to receive love free from self-loathing.

I know how to live my daily life without shame/ blame/guilt.

It is normal for me to feel no shame.

It is normal for me to feel no guilt.

I can accept it is nobody's fault.

I chose to move on with my life by releasing my past and all shame and guilt that I once carried regarding my past.

I completely release all feelings of loathing from every part of my being.

Belief work in action

Beliefs cleared:

I have to find fault in my relationship in order to improve it.

I have to find fault in myself in order to improve myself.

I blame others for not feeling the love that I desire.

I am ashamed because I do not have the relationship that I want.

Kay, a working career woman, very successful in her life yet struggled in only one area, and that area was love. Her concern was about her relationship and partner of 5 years. It is important to note that even though she was a counselor and worked closely with people, she could not see her own subconscious blocks on love. Blame and fault finding were affecting her relationship. During a particular session she was concerned about her relationship, even to the point of considering leaving the relationship because of her internal turmoil. After doing some energy work and balancing her body, Mayline proceeded to test negative beliefs that might be in the way and blocking her from moving forward in her relationship. Beliefs about blame and fault finding were the key beliefs causing her to feel stuck where she was.

Using a visual method Kay then pictured the beliefs in a sentence form written out on a chalkboard. She would then mentally erase the limiting beliefs with an imaginary eraser.

Several months later she came for a follow up session. Kay didn't even mention any difficulties concerning her relationship. Her situation almost completely dissolved and transmuted into a much more neutral place of harmony between her and her partner. She no longer felt triggered by holding onto her beliefs about finding fault in her relationship in order to improve it or needing to sacrifice herself in order to feel loved or blaming her partner for the love she wasn't receiving. She could be at peace in her relationship journey. She also commented feeling "more settled" even though she just went through a stressful move to a different state for her partner's job.

Journaling to solidify what you have learned

Guilt, blame and shame are strong motivators for behavior that limits your life. After processing your clearing work, pay attention to how your behavior changes. Record your observations below.

_____

_____

_____

_____

_____

_____

_____

We carry guilt by the bucket load, think about how your guilt has affected every area of your life. What are you ready to heal in your life where guilt once kept an open wound?

_____

_____

_____

_____

_____

_____

_____

CHAPTER TEN

ELIMINATING JUDGMENT, HATE, AND SELF DENIAL

"The greatest happiness of life is the conviction that we are loved for ourselves, or rather, in spite of ourselves." -Victor Hugo

In this chapter we focus on the emotions of hate, judgment and denial that accompany many painful situations concerning people and relationships. Certain experiences are created from your subconscious and played out in your life. When your negative perspective changes, your perceived pain from the past changes to one of a different understanding. This change in perspective is a part of the journey of healing that takes place over and over again.

The different personalities in others can trigger heightened emotional responses within ourselves. Working through heightened emotions we become more neutralized. You can then see people from a different, less judgmental place. The emotions of judgment, hate, fear or denial will only bring situations that you judge, hate, fear and deny closer in order for you to recognize that you have work to do. What do the emotions of hate, judgment and denial look like up close? The energy of denial is a particularly strong, anchored emotion of disbelief stemming from a desire to not believe a truth about something even though it is right there in front of you. It's a refusal to admit the reality of a situation. Denial provides a way of escaping from the acceptance of living from your authentic self. Facing the truth of a situation is not an easy task, even when you truly want to release your self denial.

Judgment is a broader more established set of ideas, expectations and values a person or society has about a people, places, religions or ideas. There isn't anything wrong or *bad* when you compare value, just as long as you recognize that certain value systems are created using other's beliefs not necessarily your own beliefs. To live without judgment is no small task, yet as in practicing unconditional love, we too can practice non-judgment and move into self responsibility.

Fighting Hate with Love

"Instead of hating, I have chosen to forgive and spend all of my positive energy on changing the world." -Camryn Manheim

Hate is one of the most weighted emotions. Even a small amount of hate in the form of limiting beliefs can dramatically weigh down a person's level of consciousness. For an example, have you ever felt hate towards a person you secretly admired due to some misguided fear of failure that prevented you from even trying what he or she succeeded in doing? If so, do you remember the rationalizations you made for holding on to that hate? Likely, when you were able to gain a little perspective you could see how your feelings of hate were born from your own feelings of self doubt or even unworthiness.

Perhaps you feel a little triggered by even thinking about clearing beliefs on hate. Most of us feel justified in our feelings of hate towards certain people, events or situations. Feelings of hate can be something to bond over. Think about a time that hate brought people together. 9/11 was a day fueled by hate. Hate brought destruction, death, devastation and for a time it brought people together for a common purpose. That's the funny thing about hate, it can dress up as something to unite over. The power and strength of hate is all pretend because what hate really is, is fear. Fear of what we do not understand and of the unknown.

These are beliefs that you can lay on the altar of your conscious awareness and in doing so, clear them away. Or continue to deny the strong emotions of hate for the time being only to be faced with a future situation to bring it back to be healed. That which you hate, is a mirror for something that you hate within yourself. Hearing this may be a bitter pill to swallow, but what better way to learn tolerance, kindness and acceptance? If you can uncover what about yourself you hate and clear the beliefs surrounding that perceived deficiency you will see how much more tolerant, kind and accepting you can be towards everyone.

We are placed on a path to create and encounter multiple situations that invite healing for our lives. The friend we beg to leave her abusive boyfriend, a man she both loves and hates, is learning powerful lessons in how much she hates herself. By owning that knowledge of self hatred and clearing beliefs surrounding it she could stand up for herself in self-love and in self empowerment. As much as we want to blame the boyfriend for his actions we must understand that if it was not "him" it would be another just like him until our friend can be free of self-hate.

Healing can be so painful and frustrating at times. On the physical level, a broken bone is extremely painful to be reset, yet it must be done if healing is to take place. Clearing beliefs is one way to speed up the process and provide a personal setting for healing to occur. Physical healing, emotional healing, and spiritual healing are sometimes happening at different times, but nonetheless happening all the time to one degree or another.

Ultimately, all frequencies lead to an understanding of love. God is just wanting you to listen. Are you needing to listen to your physical body? Does it need to nurtured and allowed to cleanse so your spirit can live in a more relaxed physical body? Perhaps it is your emotional body needing attention. Do you crave acceptance, or do you wish to express built up hurts to someone? Forgive all situations that cause hate. Let awareness come into your realm of being. Awareness that love is the only energy that matters. Love is what all emotional energies, even those as strong as hate, denial and fear are eventually dissolved to.

Beliefs you can clear surrounding hate, judgment and denial:

I hate spending money on needless things.
I hate myself.
I hate my own self-loathing.
I hate spending money on myself.
I hate the idea of being alone.
I hate that I can't forgive myself or others.
I have that I cannot love myself.
I hate who I am and I know everyone else hates me too.
I hate to get close to anyone, they may manipulate me in some way.
I hate trusting people.
I hate myself, therefore I am not worthy.
I hate myself because I will never be worthy of .
I hate when other people make me look bad.
I hate being in crowds.
I hate being interrupted.
I hate being slowed down by others.
I hate people that waste my time.
I hate being coerced.
I hate feeling coerced.
I hate feeling sad or uncomfortable.
I hate that people make me feel uncomfortable.
I hate people that hurt others.

I hate being over flattered.

I hate getting hurt.

I hate people that are super restricted.

I hate people that are jealous of me.

I hate people that envy me.

I hate people that compliment me because it make me feel embarrassed.

I hate people that take advantage of other people.

I hate people that hurt animals and children.

I hate people that hoard.

I hate doing anything that is not my idea.

I hate bills.

I hate and resent paying bills.

I hate doing housework.

I hate rules.

I hate going to work.

I hate/resent my job.

I hate traffic and commuting.

I hate crowds.

I hate waiting.

I hate being interrupted.

I hate dealing with people's mistakes and bad behavior.

I hate cats/dogs (insert you own.)

I hate/resent myself for not being in a place I can be close to my kids.

I hate people that are materialistic.

I hate people that have too much ego.

I hate messy people.

I hate people who can't clean up after themselves.

I hate that I'm careless.

I hate careless people.

I hate when people make me feel inadequate.

I hate that I have a hard time loving people for who they are.

I hate that my family doesn't understand me.

I hate that I wasn't taller/thinner/more attractive/smarter.

I hate that I'm aging.

I hate that I can't do what others can.

I hate that I can't do what I truly want to do.

I hate that I can't eat sugar.

I hate that men like younger women.

I hate that women like younger men.

I'm hate that I never have enough time to do the things I want to do.

I hate charging people money for my services.

I hate that people don't value what I am worth.

I hate that people don't value my time.

I hate people that don't want to have deep conversations.

I hate people because they might take advantage of me.

I hate people because they are stupid, lazy, unmotivated, undisciplined.

I hate people because they always want something from me.

I hate it when people make me feel obligated to work on them.

I hate people because they are whiny and offended about anything.

I hate to feel exposed.

I hate god for not making me feel special.

I hate that I feel that I am nothing special.

I hate that I have no talent.

I hate myself because I'm not good enough.

I hate my body because it doesn't function the way I want it to function.

I hate myself because I don't feel special.

I hate myself because I feel like a failure.

I hate myself because I feel unmotivated.

I hate myself because my life feels meaningless.

I hate people because they might take advantage of me.

I hate people because they are stupid, lazy, unmotivated and undisciplined.

I hate people because they always want something from me.

I hate it when people make me feel obligated.

I hate to be or to feel exposed.

I hate that I can not feel what other people feel.

I hate that I have to work hard for everything that I have.

I hate that I have to work so hard and others don't seem to.

I hate that people don't pay me back.

I hate when people borrow money from me and then don't pay me back.

I hate feeling obligated to loan people money or take care of them in some way.

I hate it that I feel resentment for having been taken advantage of.

I hate (certain type of) people.

I hate it when people don't help out.

I hate when people don't contribute.

I love that people contribute and help out.

I hate weddings because all of that happiness makes me uncomfortable.

I hate appearing that I'm a certain way.

I hate that I cannot trust men/women/people.

I hate that I cannot trust my family/father/mother (Insert your own.)

I hate that I cannot trust myself.

I hate my body.

I hate dealing with other people.

I would hate to have everything I want in life.

I would hate having nothing to complain about.

I would hate having free time.

Would hate to achieve my dreams and goals.

I would hate having healthy, lasting relationships.

I hate my life.

My environment has taught me that I need to hate myself and others.

Here are replacement affirmations about hate that you can tap in to replace old limiting beliefs:

I release all emotions of hate that have kept me from connecting to others.

I can allow myself to live without feeling hateful.

I release all emotions of hate that have prevented me from knowing I am connected to God and my Higher Self.

I have a bright future free from hate.

I forgive myself for having ever hated.

I forgive myself for the hatred I held in my heart.

I forgive those who have hated me.

It is easy for me to forgive others for having hurt me because I can accept they were doing the best they could in the moment.

Hate is an easy emotion for me to release.

I know how to live without hating myself or others.

I know how to live without hating God, life and world.

I know what it feels like to live my live free from hate.

It is normal for me to feel love where once there was only hate.

Love and acceptance of myself and others is growing daily in my heart.

I am in love with myself and all the world.

Our differences make us unique and I can accept the differences in others.

It is my experience that others accept my differences from them.

Limiting beliefs you can clear concerning denial:

I deny having any limiting beliefs about myself or others.

I deny that I have to experience human limitations.

I deny myself joy in order to punish myself.

I deny that I have human needs.

I deny that I must experience human despair.

I deny that I need rest like other people.

I deny having sympathy for myself.

I deny having sympathy for others.

I deny that people need my help.

I deny having any addiction.

I deny that I need other people to support me.

I deny that I need God/Love.

I must deny my own needs in order to keep the peace.

I deny my own feelings in order to survive.

I deny my inner child in order to survive.

I deny that I am selfish in establishing certain boundaries.

I deny that I feel abandoned from other people.

I have to deny and withhold love from myself to prove my worth to God and others.

I deny the stillness of my mind by keeping it occupied.

I am terrified that God will deny me his love.

I am fearful that God will deny me His forgiveness.

I am fearful that God will deny me his unconditional acceptance.

I am fearful that people will deny me their unconditional acceptance.

Other people will deny me their love and acceptance so I don't even try.

I deny myself help from others because it is my identity to be able to do everything myself.

I deny that I have any problems to work on.

To deny myself a better life will prove my worthiness.

I deny that I need anybody.

I deny that I hide from the world.

I deny that I have equal authority as men/women.

I deny that I can maintain my sense of empowerment around successful men.

I have to protect myself from my own self denial.

I have to protect myself by being in denial.

It is normal for me to live in denial.

Self denial pleases God.

My self denial leads me to greater abundance.

I deny my ability to trust that I can quit my addiction forever.

I deny my ability to trust.

I deny my ability to trust my (body, life, God, world.)

I deny my ability to trust myself to take care of myself.

I deny my ability to unconditionally trust myself.

I deny my ability to unconditionally forgive myself and others.

Replacement belief affirmations on denial:

I know how to live the rest of my life without being in denial.

I can allow myself to live without self denial.

I know longer have the need to live my life in denial.

It is safe to life my life without the habit of being in denial.

I no longer have to protect myself by being in denial.

It is normal for me to live free from self denial.

I accept a life free from denial.

I am able to move forward with complete acceptance of who I am.

I am able to move forward with complete acceptance of my past.

I am able to accept my current circumstances and acknowledge that I have what it takes to do better.

I am loved unconditionally by God, others and myself.

Limiting beliefs on judgment that you might consider clearing:

Having judgments keep me safe.

Keeping my judgments on men keep me safe.

I have to protect myself from others people's judgment.

I need to insulate myself from judgment.

I hide my true self to protect myself from judgment.

I hide my talents and abilities to protect myself from judgement.

I hide myself from the world so that I will be safe from judgement.

I have to protect myself from my families judgment.

I have to protect myself against God's judgment.

I have to protect myself against the world's judgment concerning my personal beliefs on God.

The world is a harsh and judgmental place.

I have to protect my child from the judgment of others.

I have to protect the people I love from the judgment of others.

I need to protect myself from the worlds judgment.

I have to protect myself from judgment of my past mistakes.

I don't know how to live without judging myself or others.

Judging others is all I know.

I judge others if I feel they have too much drama.

I judge others for .

I am judged for the way I look.

I am judged for my ideas.

Others judge me because .

It is normal for me to be judgmental.

Judging myself and others is normal for me.

It is my experience that I am judged harshly by others.

My judgements of others keep me safe.

I am judgmental of myself.

I am judgmental of others.

I am judgmental of others so that I don't have look at my own faults.

I judge others before they can judge me.

God stands in judgment of me.

My own family stands in judgment of me.

Others judge me.

If I show others who I am they will judge me.

I keep myself separate from others to avoid their judgment.

Being judgmental is my identity.

Being judgmental keeps me safe.

Being hard on myself and others is my identity.

I enjoy judging others and myself.

I will never be free from judgment.

People's judgments of me keep me from moving forward in my life.

It is impossible to be free from judgment.

I need to judge the world around me in order to feel safe.

I need to judge the world in order to have something to talk about.

I can't let people see who I really am because they will reject me.

I loathe people who are judgmental.

People always judge me unfairly.

Why bother, I'm not loved or understood.

I am a failure.

I deserve to be punished.

Others make me a victim.

I only know how to be a victim.

Circumstances have made me a victim and that is all I can ever be.

Being a victim is my identity.

Because I am a victim I have no power.

Because I have been a victim I will never get my power back.

I have no will to let go of being a victim.

Belief affirmations you can tap in after clearing beliefs on judgment:

I know how to live my day to life free from others judgment.

I know how to experience life feeling unconditionally accepted by people and the world.

I know how to love people free from judgment.

I know how to accept others into my heart free from judgment.

I know how to experience life without judgment.

My mind knows how to accept others into my heart free from judgment.

I can love myself despite others judgments.

I know how to live without putting myself down.

I love myself enough to quit any addiction.

I can allow myself to feel unconditionally accepted by people and the world.

I know how to live my day to day life without feeling vengeful to those who have caused me or my family injustice.

I know how to live my day to day life without the desire to destroy those who have caused me injustice.

I know how to fill my feelings of emptiness with love and fulfillment.

I know how to live my day to day life free from the world's judgment.

I can be strong and courageous in the stillness of my own mind.

I know how to embrace the stillness of my mind without distraction.

It is normal for me to live free of judgment.

It is normal for me to live free from hate.

It's safe for me to unburden myself free from judgment.

Journaling to solidify what you have learned.

Hate is hard for us to admit, yet if left to fester hate can impact our lives in a big way. Now that you have cleared beliefs on hate, in which ways have you noticed a shift in your thinking?

_____

_____

_____

_____

_____

_____

_____

What areas of life, people or situations do you hate? What areas are you still struggling to let go of hate and judgment?

_____

_____

_____

_____

_____

_____

Make a list of beliefs that come up for you that may be keeping you from expanding into new awareness concerning hate, blame and judgment.

_____

_____

_____

_____

_____

_____

The judgments you have towards others is often a mirror to what you are judging about yourself. What do you notice in others that you find less desirable? What do you notice in others that you find wonderful? Use the space below for creating your own belief statements and belief affirmations.

_____

_____

_____

_____

_____

_____

CHAPTER ELEVEN

FOSTERING LOVE AND FORGIVENESS

"Your task is not to seek for love, but merely to seek and find all the barriers within yourself that you have built against it." -Rumi

Limiting beliefs that block your ability to love create a void within you that causes one of two things: Either, you will try to hold or cling onto others in a desperate attempt to find love outside of yourself, or you will block love completely and create a wall to insulate yourself from the potential hurt love might cause should you allow it in. Those limiting beliefs that block love within you indirectly affect those who want to love and be close to you. Limiting beliefs that block love become barriers in relationships and prevent us from having more connection and intimacy we need to feel fulfilled.

Looking at the entirety of your life, you *are* loved in many ways. In moments of feeling separated, love may seem to be lost but it is fear of love that separates us. Love is what we experience when we go beyond the separation fear created in our mind. Love changes you. It is very possible to move past the illusions and perceptions you have built up causing you to doubt love.

When core love beliefs concerning God, self and others are cleared and replaced with affirmations of love of God, love of self and love of others, then an abundance of love can freely flow into your life. In this process you will realize the truth of yourself as an innately, loving and spiritual being self actualized. Clearing beliefs on love will also help you to understand love on a more intimate level within all of your relationships. At the end of each day isn't it nice to know that what the Beatles said best is true, "love is all you need."

Here are possible limiting beliefs you can clear to help dissolve blocks concerning Love:

My inner child feels unloved.

My heart is shut to protect it from harm.

I block love so that I will not be hurt.

I am addicted to the thrill of new passionate love but bail when it gets old.

When I finally love, I will inevitably be hurt/or disappointed.

I withhold love because it gets too messy.

I withhold love because I fear being vulnerable.

My inner child withholds love because he/she fears being vulnerable.

Love is complicated.

I can't love myself.

I won't love myself.

Putting myself first is selfish.

Who I am is not important.

I find myself unworthy of my own love and acceptance.

I hate who I am and therefore could never love myself.

I can't love myself unless I achieve .

I will only love myself if I am able to .

Being in love with myself is a ridiculous concept.

Falling in love with myself will do nothing to improve my life.

Loving myself will make me arrogant and unlovable to others.

Loving and accepting who I am is not a worthy goal.

I cannot receive love because I cannot love myself.

Love is ridiculous.

Love is blind.

Love is not real.

Love in not my reality.

I withhold my love and acceptance from others to punish them.

I resist all feelings of love.

It is normal for me to live blocking love in my heart.

It is normal for me to resist love.

I am incapable of love.

I don't know how to love others without giving up my freedom.

I have to give up my freedom in order to love man/others.

I must give up my freedom in order to love a child.

Others demand that I give up who I am in order for them to love me.

I have to become what someone else wants me to be in order for them to love me.

Stifling who I am is a sacrifice I have to make for love.

Because I have been a victim I will not love again.

I was victimized therefore it is not safe for me to love.

I was abused and I know I will be again if I let anyone in.

Because I have been a failure, no one can ever love me unconditionally.

All my relationships in the future will end in failure.

All my relationships in the future will end in Death.

Others are incapable of loving me.

Others are incapable of accepting all of who I am.

People are capable of deceiving me.

People are capable of betraying me.

It is normal for me to believe that all people will betray me.

Love does not exist.

Love makes you weak.

It is not safe for me to love.

It is not safe for me to give.

It is not safe for me to give; there might not be enough love for myself.

Love will be the death of me.

Love is not reliable.

It is impossible to feel love for strangers.

Love from animals is more reliable than from people.

Love is always painful.

I need everyone to love and accept me.

If I don't have everyone's approval I won't approve of myself.

Love always ends up being painful for me.

The world is unloved by God.

I am unloved by God.

I will not open my heart to love.

I block the love in my heart because I cannot trust.

I block the love in my heart because I cannot be honest with myself.

I am not ready to open my heart to love.

If I don't isolate myself, I might be manipulated.

I need to isolate myself from love in order to feel safe.

If I insulate my heart, no one will abandon or hurt me.

Loving who I am is impossible.

Loving myself is selfish.

My worth is directly related to how much others love and admire me.

I don't do things that I truly want to because if I did I might not be loved by everyone.

I do things only to gain the love and admiration of others.

I cannot love myself unless I hold a high position in employment.

My family will not love me unless I hold a high position in employment.

Love is foolish.

Lack of love is all I will ever know.

I don't know how to love.

I only love what I cannot have.

I love for all the wrong reasons.

I doubt true love exists.

It is normal for me to doubt that true love exists.

It is normal for me to be suspicious of true love.

Love is too much work.

Unconditional love doesn't exist.

I am incapable of unconditional love.

No one has ever really loved me.

I am not good enough to be loved.

No one really knows the real me, therefore no one really loves me.

There is no one out there that really loves me.

I will never fully accept and love myself.

I am not with my own love.

I am unable to release the love inside me completely.

I am not wanted.

I am not lovable.

I am unworthy of love.

Love never lasts.

I hate that I cannot love myself.

I am unable to love myself, therefore I must use escapism as an outlet.

I'm afraid of showing too much love.

I must give up my freedom in order to feel loved.

I must change who I am in order to receive love.

I must change what I look like in order to receive love.

No matter how much I try I am never loved.

There is not enough love for everyone so I will go without.

I will never be loved just the way I am.

Love always has conditions.

No matter how much I try, I doubt God's love.

No matter how much I try, I doubt myself completely.

Love is never unconditional or equal.

You have to do what others want or they will not love you.

I am afraid I won't be loved.

Love has always been withheld from me.

Everyone who loves me leaves me.

Love is pain.

When I know someone loves me I will run away.

When someone is falling in love with me, I pull away.

I have to sacrifice myself for anyone to love me.

If I care too much for someone, they will leave me.

I don't know how to love.

Love is only sexual.

I withhold love to punish others.

What's wrong with me that I can't be lovable.

There must be something wrong with me because I am still alone.

It is safer to be alone.

I'm only loved when I'm sick.

I get attention from suffering through relationships without love.

I only get loved when something goes wrong.

I only receive love when something is wrong with me.

I create problems in order to know who will love and support me.

Love is constant affection and attention.

Love is being wanted.

Love is constant passion and romance.

I need to be smart in order to receive love.

Because I doubt my own goodness, I cannot love myself.

Because I doubt my own goodness, God and others cannot love me.

I need to be sorry in order to receive love.

I need to be beautiful in order to receive love.

I am not beautiful/handsome enough to receive love.

Because I am not perfect no one can love me.

I need to be put together in order to receive love.

I need to be at my perfect weight in order to receive love.

I need to be perfect around my family in order to receive love.

I need to be perfect in order to receive love.

It broke my heart to have my trust broken.

It broke my heart to have someone I love abuse me.

If I open my heart, you might take advantage of me.

If I let someone in close to me, they may take advantage of me.

I need to insulate my feelings so my heart doesn't get hurt.

If I were truly lovable, I wouldn't have been abused.

I need to feel accomplished in order to love myself.

I need to hide my heart in order to feel safe.

It's not safe for me to emotionally connect.

If I give to someone, they might expect something else in return.

If I give too much, there won't be anything left for me.

God does not love me.

God thinks I am unworthy of loving.

God keeps me from finding love.

Positive belief affirmations on love that can replace the outdated love beliefs are:

It is possible to love again.

There is nothing I need to change about myself to deserve love.

I can learn to love.

My heart is free to experience a life free from doubting love.

I can love others free from always finding fault in them.

I want to love.

Love is safe.

It is safe for me to love.

Love is all around me.

I know how to love others without sacrificing my freedom.

I give myself permission to release all the barriers within me preventing love.

God is love.

I give myself permission to open my heart to love.

I give myself permission to give without expecting anything in return.

I can allow myself to open my heart to love.

I am a magnet to all loving relationships.

I only attract loving, honest relationships into my life.

I no longer need to worry about my appearance in order to receive love.

I no longer need to be perfect in order to receive love.

I love and accept myself just as I am.

I love and respect my parents and family, knowing our relationship has a divine purpose.

I can feel loved without constant affection.

I can allow myself to feel loved by the people closest to me.

Love radiates from me at all times.

My heart is always open to love.

Others love me with openness and acceptance.

The more I love, even more love comes back to me.

I make friends wherever I go.

Loving myself unconditionally allows me to heal.

I am love.

I am able to bypass my judgments and see love in all people.

I know what it feels like to love others without judgment or fear.

It is effortless to love without judgment.

I know how to love myself.

I accept and love myself completely.

There is nothing about me that is unlovable.

Loving myself is my first priority.

Loving myself allows me to love others more fully.

Self love and care is important to me.

I accept and love myself without exception.

I release all previous judgments of myself.

I am deeply deserving of my own love and acceptance.

I love who I am.

I am a wonderful person.

I respect myself and know how to live in a way that honors me.

I am worth loving.

There is nothing wrong with me.

There is so much love in the world.

I love myself so much.

The love I have for who I am is a great example for others.

I place myself only in situations that honor me.

I love myself just how I am.

I know how to love without fear of being abandoned.

I can love myself without suffering.

I can love others without sacrificing myself.

I can receive love without needing to be perfect.

I can receive love without needing to be at my perfect weight.

I can love others without expecting anything in return.

I can give to others without expecting anything in return.

It is normal for me to feel love and forgiveness towards others.

Its is normal for me to accept love and forgiveness for myself.

Journaling to solidify what you have learned.

Learning to love yourself is one of the most difficult challenges you will ever seek to overcome. In what ways have you been unloving towards yourself? In what ways are you loving to yourself?

_____

_____

_____

_____

_____

_____

_____

What are some of the limiting beliefs that you can clear based on your past experiences of being unloving towards yourself? Write them here and use a method of clearing that feels right for you.

_____

_____

_____

_____

_____

_____

_____

Forgiveness

"Always forgive your enemies; nothing annoys them so much. The weak can never forgive. Forgiveness is the attribute of the strong." -Mahatma Gandhi

Forgiveness is something that we become very stubborn about. Often it is confused with letting people off the hook. Sometimes you believe forgiving can make you weak. Forgiveness is not about giving permission for others to hurt you. Instead forgiveness is about you releasing yourself from the bondage of bitterness, anger, hurt and ego underneath the unforgiveness. Until you can find a way to forgive either yourself, others or the world, you are stuck with hurt and pain. One hundred percent of the time, the real victim of withholding forgiveness, is **you**.

Your physical body can also start to express unforgiveness in physical ways. Holding the energy of anger and hate can cause the body to manifest stiffness and rigidity, but it can also further manifest serious health conditions. You might very well feel justified in your anger or hate towards others, the world, your sibling that betrayed, but the unforgiveness will absolutely limit you from moving forward in your life. For those of you suffering with serious health conditions such as cancer, our best advice to you is to forgive everyone for everything, for any reason, everyday and every hour. When you forgive others you can start to heal the ego part of yourself that wants restitution for insult or injustice. Clearing beliefs surrounding unforgiveness will help forgiveness flourish.

Here are limiting beliefs you can clear that may be blocking forgiveness in your life:

I can never forgive God.

It is normal for me to stay in unforgiveness of God.

I will never forgive myself.

I will never forgive .

I will never forgive my parents.

I do not deserve forgiveness.

I continue to feel the pain of the perceived offence that I can't forgive.

It is normal for me to stay unforgiven towards myself.

It is normal for me to remain in unforgiveness of my past.

Because my spouse has not forgiven me, I am not worthy of God's forgiveness.

I block the love in my heart because I cannot forgive.

I find myself unforgivable.

I find others unforgivable.

Some people are unforgivable.

God finds me unworthy of true forgiveness.

God is un-capable of truly forgiving me.

I block the love in my heart because I cannot forgive.

I isolate myself because I won't forgive others.

I isolate myself because I believe that others can't forgive me.

I cannot forgive God if I fail.

I cannot forgive myself if I fail to provide for my family.

I block myself spiritually because I won't forgive.

There is an impenetrable barrier between myself and forgiveness.

I see myself as cynical because of unresolved unforgiveness.

I see no way to forgive so there is no way to forgive.

Only weak people forgive.

It is not in my nature to be forgiving.

Withholding forgiveness gives me power to feel in control.

I can't forgive myself because I am flawed.

I can't forgive myself because I am not worthy enough for God.

I can't forgive myself because I am a failure to God.

I am resistant to forgiving of others.

My inner child is resistant to forgiving to herself/himself.

I have made an agreement to withhold forgiveness towards others.

I can't forgive myself because I am limited by my imperfections.

My inner child can't forgive herself/himself because she is limiting by her/his imperfections.

I can't forgive myself for all of the ways I have limited my life.

I can't forgive myself for having once been so angry and fearful.

I have wasted so much of my life that it is unforgivable.

The time I wasted in anger and hate is unforgivable.

I withhold forgiveness from myself as a way to punish myself.

I can't forgive men/women because my husband/wife left me for another woman/man.

My inner child cannot forgive women/men because they rejected me.

I can't forgive women/men because my wife/husband betrayed me.

I can't forgive myself because I'm still paying penance for past wrongs.

I can't be forgiven because I've done terrible things.

I don't deserve to be forgiven for what I've done.

My inner child doesn't deserve forgiveness.

I don't deserve to be forgiven because I am an addict.

I don't deserve forgiveness because I'm a nobody.

I can't forgive myself because I am guilty.

I don't deserve forgiveness because I haven't done anything to deserve it.

If I'm a good person I deserve forgiveness, if I'm a bad person I will be punished.

I can't forgive myself for past mistakes or past choices.

People will never forgive me if I move on in my life.

My family will never forgive me for following my dreams.

I have hurt people in my life and because of what I have done I do not deserve forgiveness.

I can't forgive myself if I fail my family.

I can't forgive myself because I failed my past.

I can't forgive the past.

I can't forgive certain people from my past.

I can't forgive people that lie to me.

I cannot forgive my boss for his/her faults.

I cannot forgive myself for staying in a situation that made me unhappy.

I am willing to stay stuck in my present circumstances so that I can withhold forgiveness.

does not deserve my forgiveness.

Forgiveness will not fix anything.

If I forgive people will see it as a sign of weakness.

If I forgive people will hurt me again.

Forgiveness will not help me move on.

Forgiveness condones bad/hurtful and destructive behavior.

Forgiveness is a waste of my time.

Forgiveness has to be earned.

Something are just unforgivable.

I can't honor myself because I can't forgive myself.

I don't deserve forgiveness because my inner child is unworthy.

Because my inner child is ashamed of herself she/he can't forgive himself.

If I forgive then I won't know who I am.

If I forgive the world then I won't know who I am.

If I forgive my past, then I won't know who I am.

If I am forgiven I won't know who I am.

I don't know how to live from a place of forgiveness.

I don't know how to live feeling unconditionally forgiven.

I don't know what it feels like to be forgiven.

I will never know forgiveness.

I am afraid people would not forgive me if they knew about my past.

My past is unforgivable.

My past mistakes are unforgivable.

I can't forgive the part of myself that I continue to hide.

I can't forgive myself for feeling like a burden to the world.

My life is ruined because there is no forgiveness for me.

Because of my past failures, people/family/God may not forgive me.

I cannot forgive God for allowing me to be hurt.

I cannot forgive the world for allowing me to be hurt.

I cannot forgive myself for having done unforgivable things in the past.

I am not capable of forgiving myself for unforgivable things I've done in the past.

My heart is not capable of forgiving my unforgivable past.

I would rather die than to forgive.

I would rather suffer than to forgive myself.

Living in unforgiveness is all my heart knows.

Living in unforgiveness is all my inner child knows.

I would rather suffer than to forgive others.

I demand that God punishes those who act against me.

If God won't punish those who act against me then I will seek revenge.

I seek revenge.

Revenge must happen before forgiveness.

My enemies must be punished.

I must have revenge for .

I see no way to forgive my enemies.

Revenge blinds me.

Revenge is the only path to forgiveness.

Only when having revenge towards those who have hurt me, can I begin to heal.

I desire success only as a means to punish those who have acted against me.

I want reach my goals so I can tout my success in the faces of those who doubted me.

All else comes second to my need for revenge.

When I get my revenge, only then I can begin to forgive.

Letting go of my need for revenge is a sign of weakness.

My fight for revenge keeps me going.

Who would I be without revenge?

My heart and soul cry out for revenge against my enemies/people who have hurt me.

My enemies must suffer forever and be denied forgiveness.

I seek only total destruction of those who have acted against me.

To forgive my enemies means they win and I lose again.

My enemies will win if I forgive them.

I have no ability to forgive.

I require an apology before I can contemplate forgiveness.

I require an acknowledgment before I can contemplate forgiveness.

If I don't get a heartfelt apology I will never be able to forgive.

Acknowledgement of wrongdoing must come before I am able to forgive.

I stay insecure because I am not forgiven.

I unworthy because I am not forgiven.

I am defensive towards the world because I am not forgiven.

I live in panic and shock because the world doesn't forgive me.

I am insecure because the world doesn't forgive me.

I don't know what it means to truly feel forgiveness towards myself.

I must hide who I am because the world doesn't approve or forgive who I am.

Possible belief affirmations you can tap in to heal unforgiveness in your life:

I am secure because I know I am forgiven.

I can live my life secure and worthy of love because I know the world forgives me.

I give closure to the past, for it has no power over me today.

I forgive everyone from the past and love into the future.

Forgiveness of others does not give them power over me, it restores the power I gave them.

I can forgive all I may have wronged, past, present and future.

I give myself permission to know that God has forgiven me.

I give myself permission to know that God has forgiven others.

I know how to live my day to day life knowing that I am forgiven of all things.

I know how to forgive myself free from suffering.

I know how to forgive myself free from reliving my past.

I know what it feels like to truly forgive myself and others.

I know how to live my day to day life knowing that God forgives all people of all things.

Forgiving makes me feel liberated and free to focus on the future.

Forgiveness is my natural state of being.

I forgive myself for holding onto past injustices in order to protect my heart.

I have a habit of forgiving others quickly and moving on from my disappointment.

I know what it feels like to forgive others quickly.

I give myself permission to let go of all grudges, slights, injuries and injustices.

Forgiveness gives me another chance to show compassion.

Peace comes quickly when I can forgive quickly.

It is normal for me to stay in forgiveness towards myself and others.

It is easy for me to forgive and move past issues.

Journaling to solidify what you have learned.

Looking back upon your life, in what ways has unforgiveness prevented you from moving forward? List all people and situations.

_____

_____

_____

_____

_____

_____

After clearing the unforgiveness beliefs, what feelings have shifted? What relationships in have improved? Make a list of relationships that might still need some work.

_____

_____

_____

_____

_____

_____

_____

In a few weeks return to this journal section and recount how releasing beliefs on forgiveness has continued to open up your life.

_____

_____

_____

_____

_____

_____

CHAPTER TWELVE

OWNING YOUR POWER

"The past cannot be changed. The future is yet in your power."-Unknown.

True power comes from within, it is neither self serving nor egotistical. Truly powerful people have the ability to remain neutral in emotionally charged situations. They are the port in the storm, or the lighthouse that stands as a beacon, showing the way to the safety of the land. More than likely, they are the voice of reason and are very respected. Perhaps you have met one of these truly powerful individuals. Perhaps you have silently marveled at the way they always seem to know the right thing to say. You see, it is not the individuals who make demands of others who are powerful, it is those who have mastered their own energy in the spiritual world as well as the physical world.

Titles mean little in matters of true power. These people have mastered their internal lives achieving pure balance on the physical, mental, emotional and spiritual planes. They have great love for others, themselves, and humanity and have the ability to see beyond each moment without being consumed by the drama of the present, past, or even the future.

By clearing beliefs that limit your perspective on power, you regain a stronger sense of self and therefore create more of your own self-empowerment. Two things take away power: One is a lofty view that you are more powerful by thinking you are better than those around you, the other is placing yourself beneath others, believing that they are somehow better than you. By clearing beliefs limiting power, you can begin to understand the balance of power in your own life. What makes us powerful is that we have a mind with the ability to create and to design our own lives the way we want with our intentional thoughts and beliefs. And that is a truly *powerful* concept.

Limiting beliefs you may want to clear concerning an abuse or imbalance of power:

I'll never be satisfied as I am, I'll always want more.

I don't have a right to own my own power.

Overpowering people are intimidating.

Standing up for myself is too frightening.

I am intimidated by overpowering people.

I am timid of overpowering people.

I don't realize I am enough already.

I am too timid people do not see my as powerful in any way.

I have to escape the overpowering people in my life.

I allow others to overpower me.

I cannot stand up for myself against overpowering people.

I cannot allow myself to stand up to overpowering or dominating type people.

When dealing with uncertain emotions I am powerless.

Expressing heightened or deeply felt emotions makes me feel powerless.

Forgiving others will take away my control and therefore my power.

I am powerless to express deeply felt emotions.

My addiction has power over me.

Tv (other addiction) has power over me.

My habit of smoking has power over me.

Certain people have power over me.

My boss has all the power.

My boss has power over me.

My looks/appearance have power over others.

My prestige has power over others.

My spouse/partner has power over me.

I must have power over my spouse/partner.

Because I have no power I am afraid to speak up.

I'm afraid of harming others if I speak up.

Authorities have power over me.

Men/women have power over me.

My illness has power over me.

Food has power over me.

My work/career has power over me.

I have power over nothing.

TIme has power over me.

My lack of control has power over me.

My lack of self discipline has power over me.

I give into my apathy because I have no power.

My partner and I are not equal.

People who are desperate and helpless have power over me.

Bad weather has power over my mood.

My self sabotage has power over me.

My restlessness has power over me.

My self centeredness has power over me.

My self-recrimination of the past has power over me.

Appeasing others has power over me.

My defensiveness has power over me.

My indecision has power over me.

My lack of confidence in my writing has power over me.

My lack of confidence in my self image has power over me.

Men and women are not equal.

People with money have power over me.

I don't own my own power.

I doubt my own power.

My lack of trust in my partner has power over me.

I doubt my ability to use my own power.

My body lacks the power it did when I was younger.

Because of my health issues I lack power.

My over-protective nature has power over me.

My paranoia has power over me.

I look up to people who are in power.

I don't know how to balance my own power.

Because I doubt myself I cannot own my own power.

Because I am unworthy I cannot own my own power.

Because I am flawed/not perfect I cannot own my own power.

Because my past still haunts me I cannot own my own power.

Because my abuse still haunts me I cannot own my own power.

I have to overcompensate because I don't own my own Power.

My destructive behaviors are stronger than personal power to overcome them.

Because my past mistakes are unforgivable I cannot own my own power.

Because my addictions are so strongly ingrained I cannot own my own my own power.

I have no power over my own life.

Because I have no power I have no purpose.

Because I have been a victim of circumstance I have no power.

I have to have power over other people because I don't have power over myself.

I hate that I don't have power over myself.

Because I am ashamed of myself I have no power.

I have no power over my despair.

Abusing myself gives me power.

Abusing others gives me power.

Punishing myself give me power.

My self abuse has power over me.

I reject myself because I abandon myself.

I feel rejected because I abandon myself.

By rejecting myself I lose my own power.

Punishing others gives me power.

It's impossible to enjoy life without owning my own power.

If I cannot trust myself then I have no power.

I allow others to take away my power.

Because I'm depressed I have no power to change my life.

Because I'm unmotivated I have no power.

Because I'm sick I'm powerless.

Because I am a man/woman I am powerless.

It is normal for me to feel powerless.

Because I have no power I have no hope.

Being secure in myself gives me power.

The only relationships I have are with people who take my power from me.

Scarcity has power over me.

Money has power over me.

My fear of scarcity has power over me.

I have to freely give my power away in order to be accepted.

I am not allowed to have power.

I would not know what to do if I owned my own power.

Outside situations have the power to change my mood, feelings and thoughts.

Negative people have the power to suck me in until I feel negative too.

I allow negative situations the power to change the quality of my thoughts.

I allow negative situations the power to affect/impact my mood.

I must be addicted to something in order to avoid a relationship with myself.

I need to escape my feelings in order to avoid having a relationship with myself.

I have to seek outside myself in order to be happy.

Beliefs on rejection as a form of feeling powerless:

Because I feel rejected I have no power.

I have made an agreement with my lack of power.

Because I feel rejected by the world I have no power of my own.

It is normal to feel rejected by the world.

Because I feel rejected by (certain person) I have no power.

Because I feel rejected by (Jesus, God, Creator, Source) I have no power.

People will reject me if I own my own power.

Because I reject myself, I feel constantly abandoned; therefore powerless.

If I reject others I have power.

If I reject love I have power.

Because of my past shame, I must abandon myself.

I'm only safe when I please other people.

If I please you, you will love me.

Abusing myself causes me to reject myself.

Because I resent who I am, I neglect myself.

Resenting my past blocks me from accepting who I am today.

When I avoid my expectations I avoid failure.

If I disconnect from this person I love, I'll lose my power.

Resenting my past mistakes blocks me from moving forward.

Because I must appease others in order to keep the peace I have no power.

My judgments towards others have power over me.

Because I have no faith in myself, I have no power.

My past guilt and shame have power over me.

My lack of trust in others has power over me.

My guilt and shame over my (addiction) has power over me.

The hate of my (addiction) holds power over me.

Being worried takes away my power.

Not trusting others keeps me safe.

Trusting others with my true self would take away my power.

Trusting others takes away my power.

Because I was not protected as a child I can never learn to trust others.

Because I was powerless to protect myself, I am always afraid/worried.

Because I was not protected as a child, I don't know how to trust myself.

I would rather abandon my own needs than have the power to say no.

I have no power over my time.

My fear of people judging me has power over me

My fear has complete power over me.

The government has all the power.

My spouse/partner cannot love me if I'm in my own power.

I'm afraid to be in my own power around my partner/spouse.

I am afraid nobody will want me if I am in my own power.

The world is too messed up for me to have power over anything.

Being in my own power is too much work.

I cannot handle having any power.

I am too weak to be powerful.

I am too passive to be powerful.

I must neglect myself in order to appease others.

Others cannot know I have power or they will reject me.

It is not safe for me to own my power.

Because I must escape my feelings, I cannot relax.

Because I cannot deal with my past emotions, I cannot relax.

Because I am unable to love others unconditionally, I cannot relax.

Because I am unable to love myself unconditionally, I must reject myself.

I must reject myself because I cannot love myself.

I must reject myself because I cannot forgive myself.

I must reject others because I cannot forgive others/world.

I must reject the idea of me having any power.

The idea of death and dying has power over me.

My fear of becoming abandoned through death has power over me.

Limiting beliefs creating a negative abuse of power:

I must be in power over others because I don't have power over myself.

Money gives me power.

Money is power.

I need to insulate myself from power.

I need to be right, in order to be powerful.

I will never be accepted unless I overpower others.

If I don't have enough money, then I'm not powerful.

Being in control gives me power.

Being in control over my kids gives me power.

If I don't control others I will have no power.

My power comes from the fear of others.

There is nothing more important than being powerful.

I must be powerful in order to survive.

My professional success is more important than anything else.

I like my success to be seen.

Judging others have power over me.

Security is more important than anything else.

Money is more important than anything else.

Looking attractive is more important than anything else.

Beauty is power.

Hurting others gives me power.

Intimidating others gives me power.

Taking advantage of others gives me power.

Controlling the outcome gives me power.

I have control over the lives of others.

I am a manager/ boss so I have power over others.

I have the power to control the outcome.

I control people's livelihoods and in doing so control them.

I take power from others so they know they are less than I am.

I have earned respect through being powerful and making others afraid of me.

In order to be powerful you have to make others afraid of you.

You gain power through fear and intimidation.

I have to be better than others in order to be powerful.

I have to compete with everyone around me in order to be powerful.

I have power because I am better than everyone else.

I am the owner/boss I have power over all my staff.

My position of gives me power.

My environment has taught me that in order to be successful I have to have power over others.

My environment has taught me that life is about being powerless.

Positive belief affirmations to restore the balance of power:

I know what it feels like to live a life with balanced male/female energies within.

I have power over my fear of lack.

I have power over my fear of insecurity.

I own my own power.

I have power over the judgments I feel towards others.

I have power over my frustrations.

I am empowered in my own self.

It is normal for me to stay in my own power around others.

Because I can accept myself, I can life without rejecting myself.

I know how to stay in my own power without rejecting myself.

I let go of any and all resentment of my past actions usurping my power.

Life empowers me.

I know how to resist the pull to constantly appease others.

I have hope because I am empowered.

I can enjoy life being my empowered self.

I'm allowed to enjoy life relishing being in my own power and strength.

I know how to live my day to day life without giving away my power.

I know how to live my day to day life as a powerful expression of spirit.

I am empowered and that attracts healthy people into my life.

God works through me and is the source of my power.

I'm a valuable person in every way.

I forgive myself for believing that others have more power than I do.

I give myself permission to recognize my own power every day.

I give myself permission to recognize that have power in every situation.

I can stay in my own power in any situation and relationship.

I seek out only the conditions, situations, and relationships that support my own growth and empowerment.

I am fulfilled in my own power.

I release any and all thoughts or feelings that others have power over me.

The more choices I make for myself, the more empowered I am.

I am empowered to build a life worthy of me.

My power is my love for myself.

My power is my love for others.

My power is my authentic nature.

I can reveal my authentic self to the world and in doing so claim my power.

I have power over my fear of the unknown future.

My power is my kindness and caring towards others.

My power is my ability to forgive myself and others.

I can look my fear in the eye and take my power back.

By meeting my fear head on I have the power to release it.

I am awakened from the illusion of feeling powerless.

Journaling to solidify what you have learned.

In what areas of your life have certain behaviors or people held power over you? How do you see those behaviors or people now that you have cleared beliefs on power?

_____

_____

_____

_____

_____

_____

_____

Allow your mind to think upon past challenges that had power over you. How did those challenges transform you into the person that you are now? Come up with your own specific beliefs concerning power that you may have.

_____

_____

_____

_____

_____

_____

_____

CHAPTER THIRTEEN

CREATING CHANGE, LEARNING TO ACCEPT CHANGE, AND UNDERSTANDING COMPLETION

"Just when I think I have learned the way to live, life changes." -Hugh Prather

The one constant in life is change. However, that doesn't mean you have to like it, but what if you could accept it and understand its purpose in your life? We can all agree than that not all change is bad. Did you ever stop to think that *no* change is bad? That's right, all change serves your growth. It's what you choose to believe about change that makes it seem bad or good. Beliefs about change can run a wild gambit, strangling your mind with fear and uncertainty about the future.

People purposely stay in jobs that are unfulfilling, and relationships that are going no place simply because the idea of change is too overwhelming. Changes does create stress because people believe that it does.

Look around your life, where are you resisting change in order to avoid discomfort? Are you in a relationship that no longer serves you?

Perhaps something bigger is calling you to move in a new direction, but the very notion seems like a pipe dream. Most of the time you are oblivious to how change will serve you and the ways it will improve your life.

Clearing limiting beliefs about change can make all future changes much easier to move through. Unfortunately, you can do nothing to prevent the uncertainty of change, but you can heal yourself so that the fears concerning change will not have the power to freeze you in place ever again.

Limiting beliefs on change you might choose to eliminate:

I am uncomfortable with change.

Too much change will cause me to panic.

Too much change will me lose control.

I sabotage any opportunities that come my way.

I sabotage all change from occurring in my life.

I'm too stressed to handle anything more.

Change causes me anxiety.

Change is too hard to get used to.

New things, places and ideas are too hard to get used to.

Good things are too hard to accept.

If I allow change I will do something wrong and it will cost me dearly.

New things are stressful.

I struggle with the idea of having new experiences.

All new things and situations come with a price.

I prevent new experiences in my life to keep myself safe.

All change brings unpredictable challenges.

I don't know how to live without fear of future losses.

I have to protect myself from future losses by preventing change.

If my life changes I will miss the way it is now.

Moving forward too fast causes me panic.

When changes happen I feel out of control.

I have to be able to be in control of any changes that happen in my life.

I stand I the way of my own progress.

I stand in the way of change.

God stands in the way of change.

People in my past who have hurt me prevent me from changing.

I stay the same to make others feel comfortable.

I purposely block change because I am afraid of what it could mean.

Change is always difficult.

I cannot step into a new way of life.

I need to insulate myself from change.

Change is always scary.

Change is very stressful.

Change will cause me grief.

I will have to mourn the loss of what I have now if I change.

I am afraid/terrified of the loss that change may bring.

I have made an agreement with the fear of change.

Real change takes time.

Real change is too much work.

I live daily needing change and never seeing it.

I don't have the patience for things to continue as they are.

Lasting change is too much work.

I need to be resistant to change in order to stay safe.

I have to prepare myself for the worst.

The worst is always about to happen.

If I make a wrong decision the consequences are horrendous.

I can never get ahead.

I protect myself by not allowing change to happen.

I have have to shut down emotionally in order to get through anything.

I hate change.

I can't take any more pain or loss, so it's better to not move on.

Why bother, nothing good happens to me.

Nothing will ever change!

I am not the one who needs to change.

There is a barrier between myself and any real, positive change.

I have an impenetrable barrier between myself and change.

I will not be able to come to terms with change of any kind.

I am resistant to change.

I'm too old to change.

I am powerless to change.

I have changed enough, more is not necessary.

I'm afraid of the world so I cannot act.

I'm overwhelmed by change, so it is safer to stay where I am.

I have no purpose.

I don't have a right to choose my own destiny.

My worth is determined by the opinions of others.

Change is impossible without struggle.

I can't get any better or smarter.

Change always involves sacrifice, and I'm just not ready to do that.

Change requires being willing to let go, and I'm afraid.

I have worked so hard for change, but I never see results.

I am too stubborn to change.

I am too stupid to change.

I don't have what it takes to change.

I dont have the right education to change.

Change is too hard for me.

It is too much work to change.

If I change things it will not make a difference.

I have no will to change.

If I change, things could be worse.

It is too much work to change.

I won't like it if things change.

Why do I have to change, things aren't that bad.

There is too much pressure to change as a result I am paralyzed.

I am not responsible enough for change.

If I become unblocked then my life will change and that will be too scary and painful.

Change is scary and painful.

Change means letting go and I do not want to let go.

I have had enough change in my life I do not want anymore.

I don't really want things to change.

Change equals loss.

Change equals sadness.

I block myself from change.

I block myself from the sadness that change brings.

I couldn't change it if I tried.

It is not my responsibility to change.

I am not the one who needs to change.

I don't see how changing will solve anything.

Change will not solve anything.

I am too weak to change.

I am too old to change.

I need to change my appearance in order to be accepted by others.

It is not the right time to change anything.

The world will never change.

People will never change.

Some things will never change.

I can never get ahead because my work is always undone.

Big life changes are not safe.

I am not ready for big life changes.

I am not prepared enough for change.

It is too late for me to make changes in my life.

If I change I will be a hypocrite.

Changing things would be too unfamiliar for me.

No one will accept me if I change.

If change does not happen in the way I expect, I don't want it.

Change must only happen in a predictable way for me to accept it.

I am resistant to change.

I am resistant to transformation in all areas of my life.

I am resistant to transforming the quality of the experiences I have in my life.

I am afraid if I change I will lose myself.

I am resistant to transforming the relationships in my life.

I am resistant to transforming the relationship I have with God.

I have to be forceful with myself to exact change from within.

I must be judgemental for myself in order to change.

I should not make any changes as all my decisions are bad.

I must have a perfect plan in place before I change anything.

All conditions must be exactly right before I can allow any changes.

I am too rigid in my patterns and habits to change.

I am too comfortable with the way my life is to change.

I will not change anything unless others think I should.

Change should be minimized and controlled .

It hurts too much to think of not being a part of what I am doing in my life right now to change anything.

there is too much risk to change anything.

I am not the one who needs to change.

My happiness hinges on whether or not my can change.

I have no need to change.

Other people should do the changing.

I never make enough money to make the changes I truly want for my life.

I make excuses so that I can justify staying the same.

If I make a change it has to be small or it will be too much for me to handle.

A person cannot change their destiny.

One person is not enough to change the world.

It is my destiny to be a (fill in your label.)

Destiny can never be changed.

Destiny is set there is no changing it.

It is my destiny to be stuck in this situation forever!

I am too set in my ways to change.

I have to change myself in order to be accepted by others.

I have to change everything all the time to prevent feeling depressed or (fill in your own emotion.)

If things don't change soon I won't be able to take it.

There is nothing I can to to change my situation.

Making changes won't accomplish anything.

My family/friends will abandon me if I try to change.

I am too deeply ingrained in my situation to move on.

Moving forward is too much work.

Moving forward is too expensive.

My wont allow me to move forward.

The past is too important to let go of.

My past will dictate my entire future.

Letting go of the past means letting go of who I am.

I don't want to move forward if it means I will have to give up the comfort of the familiar.

Moving forward takes courage that I do not possess.

My current circumstances define me.

I will not know myself anymore if I change my current circumstances.

Facing an uncertain future is too much for me.

Moving forward means that I will have to leave behind too much.

My current circumstances are better than the unknown.

I cannot see a way forward so there is no way forward.

The past is more powerful than my ability to let go of it.

I am too weak to move forward.

No one can escape their past.

My patterns and habits are too strong for me to change them.

People in my life will hold me back and prevent me from moving forward.

My life is working right now, wanting more is foolish.

All change is bad, painful and a frightening.

Staying exactly the same is more likely than any change for me.

If I move forward in my life I will have to leave people I love behind.

I would have to sacrifice in order to change.

I am preventing myself from moving on because I don't want to leave behind the people I surround myself with.

It is too sad and overwhelming for me to think about moving forward.

If I move forward in my life I will make other feel left behind.

I can only be happy in relationship with my spouse/partner if he changes.

I am not the one who needs to change anything.

It is not my responsibility to change.

I can never get ahead because there is no end in sight for me.

I owe too much to ever make a change.

If I change my current circumstances I'll be out of the frying pan and into the fire.

My partner/friend is too stubborn to change.

People never change.

Old habits die hard.

Positive changes only happen to other people.

I am not lucky enough for positive changes to happen for me.

Someone else has to help me change I can't do it on my own.

I am too set in my ways to make a change.

If God wanted my life to change he would change it.

If I make changes in my life they have to be drastic changes.

Small changes are not enough for me.

If I change my mind it will make me a hypocrite.

Everything has to be perfect before change can/will happen.

Everything has to be perfect before I can/will allow change.

Everything has to be planned and perfectly executed in order for me to change anything.

I keep changing my mind and nothing ever gets done.

There are too many decisions to make for me to be able to change anything.

If everything is not perfect then I don't want to change at all.

Perfection is the only reason to change anything.

God wants me to be perfect before I see positive change in my life.

I have no choice but to stay where I am.

The choices have all been made for me.

I need someone else to make the choices.

I am unable to make changes/choices.

I have no options that I like so I will change nothing.

I just have to accept things the way they are.

If there are better ways of doing things I sure don't see them.

I can see no way to change.

There are no choices I like.

I see no choices that will lead me to the change I truly desire.

Change won't last.

Change is just an illusion.

There is no reality that I can see where changes I make are powerful and lasting.

We have always done it this way.

New ideas have no value.

A new reality is not possible for me.

I disconnect from responsibilities in order to avoid moving forward.

I am paralyzed by my fear of change.

I must restrain myself from life because I'm too afraid to change.

I restrain myself from healing fully because I am afraid to take responsibility.

I restrain my authentic self.

It's normal for me to be resistant to change.

I am resistant to leave the familiar.

I like things the way they are and I don't want them another way.

I am resistant to letting go of the structure of my life.

I won't be able to sustain this positive change for long.

Letting go of the familiar is too scary for me and I am not ready.

Anxiety and panic causes a halt in my progress.

I am helpless to make positive changes in my life.

I am doubtful in the likelihood of real change.

I have no confidence that I will be able to change anything.

There is no change that will ever satisfy me.

I can't let go of the old me.

I'll lose everything if I let go of the old me.

What I do now is my identity.

If I let go of what I do now I will not know who I am.

It is not safe to fully embrace who I am becoming.

It is not my identity to change.

It is foolish for me to believe that change can bring happiness with it.

I have to struggle in order to change.

I have built a wall around myself to protect me from change.

I am hesitant to make any changes.

I just let life happen to me instead of living on purpose.

I always hesitate to act them miss opportunities to change things for the better.

My hesitation serves me.

Reinventing myself will take too much time, energy and money.

A reinvention of my life is out of the question.

I have worked too hard to get where I am to want to think about reinventing my life.

Others can reinvent themselves but for me it's too complicated.

I need the safety net of the familiar.

A rebirth into a life I want is only a dream.

I hold tightly to the idea I have of who I am.

I hold tightly to the idea I have of who others think I am.

My environment has taught me that there is no way out of my current circumstances.

My environment has taught me that change is something to be feared.

My environment has taught me that I am trapped in my current circumstances.

My environment has taught me that I have no control over my future or what I experience.

Craving change

The flip side of needing life to stay the same, is the obsessive craving for all things to change. This goes way beyond a new shirt or rearranging the living room. This is a constant five alarm fire lit under your butt driving you to revamp your life at frequent intervals. If this scenario hits the mark for you, then read on as this next set of limiting beliefs is for you!

Beliefs on craving change that may be blocking you are:

I have no patience to wait for changes to occur in God's time.

If my life is not constantly changing I get restless.

I am driven to change everything all the time to avoid feeling restless.

I need change like I need air.

My inner child needs to run away in order to feel safe.

I need to change in order to feel safe.

People around me hold me back from changing and I resent them for it.

Change or die.

I feel stifled if I am not changing constantly.

I am not content if things remain the same for too long.

No one can keep up with me.

I crave change.

I am obsessed with changing.

I desire change to the point of obsession.

If I change everything all the time I will not have time to sit with my pain.

Constant change prevents me from dealing with my past and my hurt.

I use change as way to make up for the wrongs of my past.

I use change as a distraction.

Change for the sake of change is enough.

I feel oppressed if I have to keep things the same for too long.

No one in my life will allow me to change in the way I truly need to.

If I make a change, it has to be big or it will not matter.

I am desperate for change.

I am desperate to move forward.

It drives me crazy to stay in one place long.

I need to keep moving.

If things don't change for me I won't be able to stand it anymore.

I can't continue a moment longer without change.

Change has to be all or nothing.

Change for the sake of change is better than nothing.

If change does not happen the way I want it then I don't want it at all.

I can only be happy if changes happen all the time.

Completing what you have started

Completion is a type of change that carries both joy and grief wrapped up in a confusing package. When the time has come to move on from something, the change can bring up feelings of loss. Completion can also bubble up fear related to your project being judged. If you are experiencing heartache brought about by the end of a project, or a relationship then the following limiting beliefs are for you.

Limiting beliefs blocking completion that you could clear are:

My project is nearly complete I don't know what I will do when I no longer have it to work on.

I fear completing my education because then I will have to find a job in my field and I don't know if I will.

My job is almost complete I won't know how I will support myself when it is done.

I stay in projects longer than I need because I am uncomfortable with the finality of completion.

When situations come to an end I am saddened.

I will lose the people I have worked with when this project ends.

It's too sad to ever complete anything.

I never want to finish my project.

If finish my project then other people will judge it.

What if I never complete my project?

What will it mean for me if I finish my project?

I don't know what to do now that my project is complete.

I am afraid that if I complete my lessons I will no longer recognize myself.

I am too afraid of the unknown to complete my work.

If I move on or start something new I might regret it.

I won't know what to do with my time if I finish my work.

People will reject me if they don't like my completed project.

If my project is never completed then I cannot be judged.

I don't know how to finish my project.

I don't want to start something new because I'm always disappointed.

I am intolerant towards my own future fears of failure.

Completion is so final that is scares me.

I am never satisfied with my completed work.

Because my relationship has ended, I'm a failure.

I'm afraid to admit my relationship has reached its' completion.

Because there was no closure to my relationship, I am incomplete.

Belief affirmations for Creating change:

Just like your imagination can turn shadows in the dark into ferocious monsters, so can your beliefs about change. A distorted idea of change can give it power over you. Now that you have made room for new ideas about change to occur, you can really start to live with a new understanding of how your thoughts create your reality. Get ready to create a reality of light so bright that no monster would dare creep too close, by tapping in the beliefs in the following section.

Belief affirmations you can use for creating change:

I am a child with a destiny and a purpose.

I am a champion of change.

I choose to break the family patterns and create better ones for myself.

I trust myself and others.

It is normal for me to trust myself and others.

The best is always about to happen.

I am willing to receive all the positive benefits of moving past my self destructive behaviors blocking change in life.

I give myself permission to move forward in life.

I give myself permission to grow beyond my family's expectations.

It's safe for me to move forward without fear of future losses.

My current circumstances are not my future.

I can completely let go of the old me.

I am choosing ways to be successful and I feel self satisfaction and love.

I am blessed with positive light energies.

I give myself permission to move forward with ease and effortlessness.

I have a right to explore my possibilities.

I have a right to express my needs and desires in an appropriate way.

I am aware of the negative but I choose to focus on the positive.

I have my own worth and I choose to be the person I want to be.

I am recognizing the compensations I've been given.

I know how to be busy with change yet not be overwhelmed.

I can change without being overwhelmed.

I know how to live my life without being terrified by change.

I know how to create for myself despite outside disorder.

I can accept myself despite the changes within me.

Change equals newfound freedom.

I am adapting everyday.

Change is good because I am adaptable.

My ability to adapt to change is marvelous.

I am ready to adapt to new, positive ways of living.

Adapting is natural for me.

I am a master at adapting to change.

I release all fear about change and my ability to be successfully adapt.

My mind easily adapts to change.

My body easily adapts to change.

I surrender to the change I have been waiting for.

I can release my control that prevents change.

I can release my disconnect that prevents change.

I know how to live my life without limiting beliefs.

I can allow my inner child to move forward with ease and freedom.

I know how to live a life free from limiting beliefs.

I am free to move forward in health and harmony.

I am in harmony with the thoughts I think concerning my future.

I am in harmony with the thoughts I think towards my past.

I am in harmony with change in my life.

I am in harmony with the change I see in the world.

It is safe allowing myself to complete projects.

It is safe for me to make positive changes in my life and move forward from unhealthy relationships and situations.

I am excited and happy to be done with my current job and to move on to the next one.

It is normal for me to be at ease with the positive changes I see for myself in the future.

I can let go of old beliefs of who I thought I was so that I can step into who I really am.

I release all thoughts that I have to live up to what others think I am.

I release all that I was.

It's safe for me to completely let go of who I have been.

I am ready to let go of the "old" me.

I am excited to embrace my new experiences.

There is joy in releasing the old to make room for the new.

It's acceptable to me to step into the unknown because I fully trust that God is guiding my way.

I let go of all that was so both hands are free to grab hold of all that I am becoming.

Habitual ways of thinking and being in the world and in my private life are unraveling and I am at peace with this.

It is normal for me to be excited about the future.

I am open to receiving all the benefits of releasing the "old" me.

I am open to receiving all the benefits of becoming the new me.

In the future all things are possible.

Great joy and contentment are on the way to me.

I decide right now to completely let go of my past.

I decide to take the lessons of my past and let the rest go.

I will not fail.

God will not let me fail.

Even if things don't go as planned it doesn't mean that I have failed.

I am empowered to release my old stories, beliefs and expectations.

I am empowered to believe in myself and my strength and my courage.

I am empowered by God.

I give permission to God to help guide me through the changes I need to make.

Change can occur peacefully.

I release all fears that change is stressful and difficult.

There is nothing to fear.

There is nothing wrong.

There is nothing to fix.

Life is change.

Life is growth.

I live my life on my terms.

There is only to allow, to release and to repeat.

I gracefully accept all the lessons from change that may occur in my life.

It is safe for me to use change in a healthy way to create the life I dream of.

I can allow change to create a bright future for me.

It is so easy for me to make healthy, positive changes in my life.

I accept the pace of changes and allow them to occur in the perfect time.

I release all need to control the changes that happen in my life.

I am adaptable.

I am resilient.

I am creating a future worthy of me.

I welcome positive changes to flow into my life now.

It is safe for me to be done with certain situations, people and projects in my life.

I free myself from the fear of judgement and my work or the changes I wish to make.

It is my life to live and I can move forward empowered to live it more fully.

I have awakened from the illusion of having no control of my experiences.

Journaling to solidify what you have learned.

What purpose does keeping things the same serve for you? What beliefs surround the need to stay put that prevent healthy change and growth?

_____

_____

_____

_____

_____

_____

_____

What things in your life do you seek to escape from instead of moving forward?

_____

_____

_____

_____

_____

_____

_____

How far could you move forward now that you have the tools to create change for yourself? Make a list of the things you will change in your life now that you know you have the freedom to do so.

_____

_____

_____

_____

_____

_____

_____

Who would you be if there were no limits to on what you could become. How would you design your life?

_____

_____

_____

_____

_____

_____

_____

CHAPTER FOURTEEN

CREATING THE ABILITY TO ALLOW AND TRUST

"I like knowing that whatever I am willing to ALLOW, the Universe will yield it to me." -Abraham Hicks

We block ourselves from allowing positive experiences by adopting limited perceptions that we believe define us. We create endless excuses to avoid that which we do not trust out of fear of being disappointed. Doing all the right things, such as visualization, affirmations, vision boards, meditation, and prayer and not seeing results can cause you doubt. The feeling of doubt becomes distrust which denies you the positive experiences you are yearning to have. Giving up on dreams stems from a place of distrust when all that is needed is to simply *allow*. If you don't allow for things to things to show up in the way that is best for you, then you could be blocking the things you really want, because they weren't showing up the way you expected.

Allowing is our natural state of being. Think about a child and their sense of wonder, curiosity, and enthusiasm for play. Play at allowing. Find joy in opening up to what the future can hold. Clearing beliefs that block the ability to allow and to trust, will help you to experience wonderment, amusement and will open your life in a big way.

Limiting beliefs blocking the ability to allow positive change into your life could be:

I cannot allow myself to relax.

It is normal for me to feel stressed.

I cannot allow myself to relax without (alcohol, Tv, internet,etc.)

I cannot allow my life to change for the better.

If I allow all of the good that wants to come to my life people will be jealous.

God will never allow me to be happy.

My family will never allow that to happen.

My family will never allow me to feel accepted.

My (insert your own relationship) will never allow me to be happy.

God will never allow me to experience peace in my life.

I do not allow myself to live a life of ease.

It has to be more complicated that to just allow.

I am not allowed to live my life the way I want to.

I am not allowed to change.

I will not allow myself to forgive.

I do not allow myself to be forgiven.

I do not allow myself to give and receive love.

I do not allow myself to have healthy and loving relationships.

I do not allow myself to be free from suffering and the weight of fear.

I do not allow myself permission to move on.

I do not allow myself to be successful.

I do not allow myself to experience financial security.

I do not allow myself to let go of control.

I do not allow myself to let go of emotional control.

I do not allow myself to feel the full effect of God's love for me.

I do not allow myself to feel love for myself.

I do not allow myself to feel the love from others.

I do not allow myself to believe that my life can change for the better.

I do not allow myself to expect good things to happen to me.

If I allow myself to experience joy I will be disappointed.

If I allow myself to experience abundance, I will feel guilty.

My subconscious mind does not allow healing methods to work for me.

My inner child will never allow me to heal and grow.

My inner child will never allow me to live without my habits.

I can't allow my subconscious to live without my ego.

Allowing good into my life is impossible.

Allowing abundance into my life is out of the question.

Allowing my dreams to come true is not something I am willing to do.

Allowing myself to reach my goals is not something I really want.

If I allow myself to embrace leaving my current job, everything will be ripped out from under me and I will lose all the ground I had gained.

I have put too much effort into the life I have to allow change even for the better.

God does not want to allow me a peaceful and easy life.

If I allow myself to have a peaceful and easy life something will happen to take it away.

If I allowed all positive change to happen, I would not be able to handle it.

Allowing is too scary for me.

Allowing is not possible for someone of my station in life.

Allowing will not help me in any way.

Allowing will make things too easy for me and I don't deserve positive change.

I am not meant to allow good things to happen for me.

Allowing will not fix anything.

Allowing is something that I just cannot do.

Allowing is too easy it needs to be more difficult in order for the change to be accepted.

I feel guilty for not allowing love in my life.

I feel guilty for not allowing people to love me.

I feel guilty for not allowing myself to love others.

I feel guilty for not allowing myself to love myself.

I feel guilty for not allowing forgiveness and love to take the place of blame and hate.

I am not allowed to ask for help.

I am not allowed to make mistakes.

I am not allowed to be my authentic self.

I am not allowed to feel angry, frustrated, sad or upset.

I am not allowed to give myself a break.

No one is allowed to make mistakes that affect me.

I will not allow myself to be vulnerable.

Allowing will not change anything.

I am doomed no matter what I allow.

I allow only negative things and people in my life.

I do not allow God to love me.

I do not allow myself to be provided for.

I feel guilty allowing others to help me.

I do not allow Divine assistance in my life.

I allow pain and suffering to be my only truth.

I can't allow myself to move on because I will only let people down.

If I allow myself to have high expectations in life, I will only be disappointed.

I expect to reach my goals in exactly the way I have planned.

If my expectations are not met then I will not accept what comes my way.

If my expectations are not met then I am angry, frustrated and disappointed.

I am a slave to my own expectations.

I am a slave to the expectations of others.

I will never live up to my 's expectations of me.

I will never live up to God's expectations.

If life does not go the way I expect then I can't handle it.

I am frustrated by the pressure I feel from others expectations of me.

I am frustrated by my own expectation.

If people don't behave the way I expect I get angry/upset.

I am tired of never living up to my own expectations.

I am tired of never living up to 's expectations.

It is enough to expect my life to change, I don't have to put in any effort.

It is my expectation that everything go according to plan.

The unexpected is scary.

The unexpected causes me stress.

The unexpected of the past causes me stress.

The unexpected of the future causes me stress.

I am too rigid in my expectations to allow for life to flow differently.

I expect myself to be able to carry all the responsibility alone.

I expect myself to behave perfectly and to never make mistakes.

I expect everyone to behave perfectly and never make mistakes.

I don't have enough resources in my life to move forward.

I have too many responsibilities to move forward.

No matter what I do it feels difficult to move forward.

Belief affirmations to tap in for using allowing to your advantage:

I allow God to work miracles in my life.

I allow for the possibility of a prosperous life.

I allow for a healthier, happier outlook on life.

The truth is that I do allow all the good God wants to give me.

The truth is that it is easy for me to let go of that which no longer serves my growth.

The truth is that I deserve happiness and harmony in every aspect of my life.

I allow myself to accept the truth, that I am one with all of Divinity.

I allow myself to accept the truth, that all humanity is one with Divinity.

I allow all my dreams to come true.

God allows me to be fulfilled.

I allow myself a life of love and fulfillment.

I allow myself to let go of things that no longer serve my growth.

I allow myself to let go of people who are not in alignment with how I want my life to be.

I allow others to help me.

I allow myself to accept help from others.

I allow my life to be filled with wondrous surprises.

I allow my life to be filled with grand adventures.

I allow myself to be in a state of positive expectation.

I allow myself to embrace change.

I am allowing me to be exactly who I am in every moment.

I believe that I can allow all of my dreams to be achieved.

I allow changes to take place in my life that lead me to a bigger life than I can imagine.

I release all fear surrounding allowing change, growth and abundance into my life.

The truth is that I can graciously receive all the good that change brings.

I am liberated from my former ways of being in the world.

I am liberated from my former habits and habitual ways of thinking.

I am liberated from my former ways of seeing myself, others and the world.

I am liberated from my former blocks.

I am liberated from all former barriers to a deep connection to God.

I am liberated from all former patterns.

I am liberated from all my former limits.

I am unlimited.

I am unhindered.

I am free to live a bigger life than I was able to see before.

I am free from all restrictions, boundaries and blocks to the life I want.

I am free from all of my former patterns of behavior, habits and ways of thinking.

I am an open vessel for Divine energy to work through.

I am open to new ideas and ways of living.

I can allow myself to believe that relationships are free from complexity.

I can allow myself to live without the restraint of the expectations I place upon myself.

I can allow others to live without preconceived expectations.

It is not my job to please other people in life.

I can live my truth without the fear of others' judgements or expectations.

I know what it feels like to live a life free from experiencing judgment.

It is safe for me to enjoy other people without a sense of expectation and judgment.

It is safe for me to enjoy society without expectation or judgement.

I can allow myself to enjoy society without expectation or judgement.

I am willing to receive all the positive benefits, such as joy and peace that come by living without judgment.

I can recognize the person I can become, when living freely without limitations, judgements and expectations.

Because we cannot allow that which we do not trust, beliefs on trust are listed below for you to clear.

Limiting beliefs blocking trust:

Trust is an illusion.

Trust is a lie.

If I trust then I will be a fool.

I have trusted and been hurt in the past so I resist trusting now.

I resist trusting others.

Others resist trusting me.

I am confused about what to trust.

Trusting is painful.

Trusting takes time.

Nobody trusts me.

I need to dominate people because I don't trust them.

Because I don't trust myself I need to control everything.

Because I don't trust others, I need to control everything.

I have no trust in myself.

I have no trust in the people around me.

I have no trust in my ability to navigate through my life.

I have no trust that my life will expand in a positive way.

I have no trust in positive beliefs.

I have no trust in clearing beliefs.

I have no trust I will ever be happy.

I have no trust in money.

I have no trust in my ability to make money.

I have no trust in my relationships.

I have no trust in life.

I have no trust in the longevity of love.

I have trust issues.

I can't trust myself to be vulnerable around people that I love.

I can't trust marriage.

I cannot trust men/women.

I can't trust what people do or say.

I cannot trust life.

I can't trust God to support me.

I can't trust that my life will work out the way I want.

I can't trust that allowing is enough.

I can't trust that I am enough.

I cannot trust people will do the right thing.

I cannot allow myself to trust.

I can't trust that it is safe for me in the world.

I cannot trust that family will be there for me when I need them.

I can't trust that my life will continue as it is without my control.

I can't trust that God will provide for my needs.

I can't trust to let go of my own control.

I can't trust that people will meet my expectations.

I can't trust that I won't meet my own expectations.

I can't trust that I can truly forgive others.

I cannot trust my intuition fully.

I can't trust that I can truly forgive myself of the past.

I can't trust that people will be there for me when I need them.

I can only trust myself.

I can only trust those that constantly prove themselves to me.

If people want my trust they must consistently prove themselves.

I cannot trust God fully.

My lack of trust in people is all that I know.

My lack of trust in the world is all that I know.

My lack of trust in myself is all that I know.

My lack of trust in the world is normal for me.

My lack of trust in people is normal for me.

My lack of trust in my ability to create is normal.

My lack of trust is finishing my work to completion is normal for me.

I only trust in the data and logic that is in front of me.

I trust that people and the world will eventually betray me.

I trust that people and the world will eventually fail me.

I only trust in the dark side of human behavior.

I only trust that I can and will continue to attract negative people and situations.

I only trust in lack and scarcity.

I only trust that I will never have enough.

I only trust that I will never be enough.

I only trust in what I can see.

I only trust in the darkness with in my own soul.

I only trust that people will hide the truth from me.

I only trust that people will hurt me eventually.

I only trust that people will lie.

I only trust that I can feel safe by lying.

I only trust pain.

My inner child uses lack of trust in order to live.

My truth is that life is hard.

My truth is I have to struggle.

My truth is that fears keep me safe.

My truth is that my fear of marriage has power over me.

My truth is that I must struggle to sleep.

My truth is that I must struggle with addiction.

My truth is that I will never be free from my limits.

I must lie because I do not know what my own truth is.

My truth is all relationships are hard, complex and difficult.

My truth is that having children is hard work.

My truth is that having children is painful/difficult.

My truth is that becoming pregnant/fertile is difficult.

I don't trust that I live from my authentic self.

I don't trust that I can give what my partner needs.

I don't trust in the longevity of love.

I don't trust that people are who they say they are.

I don't trust in the worlds ability to accept me.

My heart doesn't trust life.

I trust that my my mind is capable of healing my body from anything.

I deny my ability to trust that I can quit my addiction forever.

I deny my ability to trust.

I deny my ability to trust my (body, life, God, world)

I deny my ability to trust taking care of myself.

I deny my ability to unconditionally trust myself.

Because I can't trust others with my true authentic self, I can't connect with them.

Because I can't trust myself to be my true authentic self, I cannot connect with anyone.

I am not able to trust and keep promises to myself.

Belief affirmations encouraging trust that you can tap in:

I accept in my ability to unconditionally trust myself.

I trust in my ability to trust God.

I have complete trust in my ability to complete my work.

I trust in my ability to finish my projects.

I have full trust in the world to accept who I am.

I trust that the world believes in who I am.

I trust that the world has faith in me.

I have full trust in knowing my family is there for me.

I have full trust that my partner will understand what is in my heart to do.

I trust that the world will forgive me unconditionally.

I trust that God will forgive me unconditionally.

I trust that my partner will forgive me unconditionally.

I trust that I can feel safe and free from the need to lie.

I trust that I can feel safe eating all food free from reactions.

I trust that I am enough.

I can trust in my ability to truly be happy for people and their progress.

I trust that people are enough.

I trust in my ability to create healthy boundaries.

I trust in my ability to say "no."

I trust in my ability to only think and create positive thoughts.

I trust that all people are truly kind and good.

I trust that I am truly kind and good.

My truth is that having children is beautiful and amazing.

My truth is that relationships can be easy and flowing.

I trust that I can experience a painless (childbirth.)

I have total trust in my ability to allow my dreams to come true.

I have total trust in myself and in all of my relationships.

I have total trust in God's desire to support me.

I have total trust in life.

I have total trust in the good in all people.

I have total trust my life will unfold in a wonderful and magical way.

I have total trust in God.

I have total trust in my dreams.

I have total trust in my talent.

I trust that I live from my authentic self.

I trust that I am healed.

I trust in my unlimited nature.

I trust in the longevity of unconditional love.

I trust my that people in my life are truthful with me.

I trust in the light that is in my soul.

I trust in the light that is in the world.

I trust that lightness and joy is sustainable for me.

I trust that love and peace are sustainable for me.

I trust that my goals and dreams are attainable.

I trust in a positive outcome for all of my endeavors.

I trust all will go smoothly in my day to day life.

Trust in myself is normal for me.

Trust in the world is normal for me.

Trust in my relationships is normal for me.

Trust in getting all I desire that is in my highest good is normal for me.

I release all distrust from every part of my being.

I release distrust from my heart and allow love to heal me.

I easily trust the choices I make and the direction I am going.

Being trustworthy is my natural state.

Being trusting is my natural state.

I can be trusting and safe.

I can see when people are not truthful with me and understand they are trying to protect themselves.

I can work through all moments of distrust in a painless and easy way.

Having trust is safe.

Journaling to solidify what you have learned.

Allowing isn't difficult, but shedding the fears and habits blocking allowing can sometimes be difficult to release. What have you been afraid to *allow* into your life because of hesitation or stinginess?

_____

_____

_____

_____

_____

_____

_____

What dreams have been boxed away for *someday*? Write them down and create a list of things you intend to *allow* and *trust* that what you desire will to come into your life with ease.

_____

_____

_____

_____

_____

_____

Trusting opens up your life in ways that may be surprising. In the coming weeks, revisit this section and expand on the areas where trust might remain an issue for you. Create different trust beliefs that are personal to you here:

_____

_____

_____

_____

_____

_____

_____

CHAPTER FIFTEEN

MAKING ROOM FOR FAITH AND CERTAINTY

"Now faith is the substance of things hoped for, the evidence of things not seen."

Hebrews 11:1, KJV

Our relationship with faith continues to unfold throughout our entire lives. At times faith is a rock, keeping us from losing ourselves in a torrent of trials or tragedy. Other times, faith leaves us feeling like a scorned lover, bitter and betrayed when it is lost. However you feel about faith in this moment, chances are that you have known faiths' opposite which is rational belief built upon ideas of logic and data. The concept of faith is a strong trigger for many. Those who have faith feel they must defend it. And those who have lost faith, can feel there is no point to any of this business we call life.

Faith simply means believing something is true and then committing our lives to it. However, experiencing a strong sense of faith and a strong belief are quite different. Many limiting beliefs, such as, "I have lost my faith in humanity," are firmly held by people. Faith is of utmost importance in understanding that your beliefs help to shape your faith in various areas of life. That is especially true when it comes to dealing with many ideas about the world around you. Where do you place your faith? And how do positive beliefs help you to work on building your sense of faith?

By now, you've learned that beliefs are a product of your subconscious mind. Your beliefs can be altered throughout life by your experiences. Regardless of the beliefs that affect how your mind views the world, it has nothing really to do with your spiritual heart. The heart understands a connection with God and universal energy. Faith is the result of being in-tune with your heart despite the chatter of your ego that seeks to isolate and protect itself by creating rationality and disconnecting instead. It is the responsibility of your heart to truly experience and to know where to place your faith.

To have faith is about stepping into alignment with your inner knowingness. Your job is simply to do your best in the moment, and to experience the faith of knowing that you are working from your understanding of the truth, as it comes from the heart.

The heart experiences the world far differently than the mind. When the heart knows, there is no room for fear. Without faith, fear in the form of limiting beliefs will always find its way into your heart. Strengthen your faith by clearing limiting beliefs.

Limiting beliefs on faith you can clear for yourself:

I lack faith in myself.
I have no faith concerning my self-worth.
I lack faith concerning the future
I lack faith that I will be well again.
I lack faith in my body's ability to stay strong and healthy.
I have no faith in being seen as a professional.

I have no faith in being seen as a (lawyer, doctor, actor, etc.)

I lack faith concerning my ability to see a difficult project through to its completion.

I have no faith is my ability to give affection others.

I lack faith concerning my ability to finish a project.

I lack faith concerning my ability to push through difficult situations.

I lack faith concerning my ability to trust.

I lack faith in my ability to eat certain foods.

I lack faith in a higher power.

I lack faith in love.

I lack faith that others would be there for me in the future.

I lack faith that my partner would support me in the future.

I lack faith that my partner would be supportive of my emotional needs.

I lack faith in my ability to finish my project.

I lack faith that I will be successful in the future.

I lack faith that I will have energy in the future.

I lack faith that God/Higher Self will sustain me.

I lack faith in my willingness to change.

I lack faith that I will sleep soundly in the future.

I lack faith in the goodness of people.

I lack faith in the goodness of this world.

I lack faith that I can protect myself from darkness/evil.

I lack faith that I can experience a life of peace

I am resistant concerning my own faith in a higher power.

I have no faith in people because I fear them.

I lack faith in people because I have been betrayed.

Because I have been betrayed, I have no faith.

Because God betrayed me, I have no faith.

I lack faith in my ability to control my addictive nature.

I'm afraid people will lack faith in my abilities.

I lack faith that I will grow old.

I lack faith that I will live past a certain age.

I lack confidence in my ability to have faith in a higher power/ myself/people.

I am doubtful of those who have faith.

I am doubtful of my own faith in .

I lack faith in marriage.

Being faithless is all that I know.

I only have faith in myself.

I lack faith in my body's ability to heal itself.

I lack faith that I can heal my relationships.

I lack faith that my relationships can be healed.

There is so much hatred in the world I have no faith that it can be healed.

I am uncertain in my ability to have faith in myself.

Things never work out for me.

Just when I think things are going well, the rug gets pulled out from underneath me.

I have no faith that life can be fun or easy.

I have no faith in my abilities.

I have no faith in God or my Higher Self.

I have no faith in the divine.

I have no faith that I will get any help from divinity.

God has no faith in me.

The world has no faith in me.

I do not believe anyone should have faith in me.

I have no faith in my ability to achieve my dreams or goals.

I will never have enough faith.

The world will never have enough faith.

Faith is worthless.

I have no faith in other people.

I have no faith in humanity.

I have no faith in politicians.

I have no faith in world leaders.

I have no faith that people can change.

I have no faith that anyone will really help me.

I have no faith that anyone can help me.

I have zero faith that I can help myself.

I have no faith in peace or happiness.

I have no faith in that which I have not experienced.

No one, not even God, has earned my faith.

I have not done enough to earn the faith of anyone, even God.

I have no faith that there is a God or a Heaven.

There is only life, death, then nothingness.

I have no faith in the ability of others to do what is right.

I have no faith my life will work out the way I want.

No one has faith in me.

I can have no faith in myself.

I have no faith in what I want.

Faith is a myth.

Faith has no basis in reality.

It is foolish to have faith.

I have no faith that I will ever discover my true purpose.

I have no faith that people in the world can get along.

I have no faith in my relationships.

I have no faith in my marriage.

I have no faith in marriage.

I have no faith in abundance.

I have no faith in my dreams.

I have zero faith in myself.

I set goals, but have no faith that I will achieve them.

I don't bother setting goals; I'll never achieve anything.

Nothing I do comes out right.

I will always feel the emptiness of having no faith.

I will always feel the emptiness of being disconnected from my faith.

By having no faith, I will not be disappointed.

If I have no faith, I won't be disappointed in myself.

I will always have to work hard; therefore, I have no faith in things that come easy.

I am only certain of failure.

I am certain that I have no worth or value.

I am certain that I will fail.

I am certain I will die young.

I am certain I will never be successful.

I am certain that if I show the world who I really am, I will be rejected.

If I allow people to know who I am, I am certain they will reject me.

I am certain I will be abandoned by everyone, including God.

I am certain that God punishes me by making me suffer.

I am certain that I will be harmed if I let others see who I really am.

There is no certainty for me.

There is no certainty that I will be around for my children.

There is no certainty that anything will work out.

I am certain that mankind will destroy itself before anyone can conceive of taking the high ground.

I am certain the world is a harsh and dangerous place.

I am certain the world is full of disappointment and pain.

I am certain the world is full of deceit and lies.

I am certain I will find the same problems over and over.

I am certain I will deal with the same relationship challenge over and over again.

I am certain that I am stuck in this endless loop of despair that is my life.

I am certain only of things that I can prove scientifically.

I am certain only of things that I can see and touch.

I am certain only of the physical world.

I am certain that people are worthless and disgusting.

I am certain that people are not capable of doing anything that is good and kind.

I am certain that people are evil and capable of unimaginable harm.

No one can be certain of anything except death and taxes.

I am certain I will continue to suffer in my life.

I am certain people will continue to have no faith in me.

My environment has taught me that having faith doesn't serve me in any way.

Here are some beliefs affirmations you can use to fortify faith and certainty:

I have faith in myself.

I have faith in God's love for me.

I have faith in a higher power.

I walk daily with faith.

It's normal for me to be certain in myself.

It's normal for me to live with faith.

I have faith in my abilities.

I have faith in clearing beliefs.

I have faith that I can provide for my loved ones in the future.

I have faith that I will be provided for in the future.

I have faith that my past will never haunt me again.

I have faith I can stop smoking.

I have faith I can be at my ideal, healthy weight.

I have faith that my partner and I will create a happy life together.

I have faith that I will be protected while sleeping through the night.

I have faith in my ability to sleep.

I have faith that I will be sustained by a higher power.

I have faith in my ability to trust myself.

I have faith in my ability to trust others.

I have faith in my ability to make right decisions.

I have faith that I will know when to let go and when to take control.

I have faith that I can do the right thing.

I have faith in my ability to quit my addiction.

I have faith in my ability to say no with ease and grace.

I have faith in my ability to take care of myself.

I have faith in my ability to take care of loved ones in the future.

I have faith that people will not judge me for my beliefs.

I have faith that all things are possible.

My faith inspires others.

My faith in the future shines brighter every day.

I welcome faith in myself, God and others into my life.

I give faith the freedom to grow in my life.

I have faith that my dreams are on their way to me.

I have faith that I have always been and always will be enough.

I have faith that joy is filling up all the days of my life.

My goals are worthy of my faith.

I am certain that all things are possible.

I am certain I am attracting people who will help me reach my goals.

I am certain of my faith in myself.

Everything in my life works out for the highest good.

Feeling certain of myself is normal for me.

I am certain of a peaceful and abundant future.

I am certain of continued health.

I am certain in my relationships.

I am certain all things are possible.

I am certain of my dreams and the direction I want to go.

I am certain of my purpose.

I am certain God/Higher Self guides me on my way.

I am certain of my place in the world.

I am certain that mankind is capable of great love.

I am certain of my strength and ability to adapt to change.

I am certain that I am ready for a change.

I am certain that I can face any challenge with grace and courage.

I am certain of my diligence.

I am certain of my will to succeed.

Journaling to solidify what you have learned

Faith ebbs and flows throughout our lives. Remember the moments your faith was shaken. What emotions were present? Now remember moments where you had absolute faith. How did you feel in those moments? How has you work in this chapter helped you make room for more faith?

_____

_____

_____

_____

_____

_____

Having certainty is rare and may only have felt available to you around certain subjects. Now that you have an expanded awareness of certainty what subjects are you feeling more certain about?

_____

_____

_____

_____

_____

_____

_____

CHAPTER SIXTEEN

SURRENDERING AND RELEASING FOR A WORLD WITHOUT LIMITING BELIEFS

"What lies behind us and what lies before us are tiny matters compared to what lies within us. And when we bring what is within us out into the world, miracles happen."

-Ralph Waldo Emerson

No matter the pace at which you have made your way through this workbook, you have now arrived at what is the end of one chapter of life and the beginning of another. A whole new level of expansion happens when you are able to choose how you want to live by creating new beliefs about any situation. Your world is growing internally and externally. By now, all the limiting beliefs you have cleared thus far is more like entering the garden of Eden, one that now fully supports the individual you have become. Every option and experience is available to you. Like a giant buffet line, life is stretching before you. There are plenty of choices available and for everyone else as well. Simply leave on the table any limiting beliefs you don't want to clear or that is not necessary for your unique situation.

The more you clear away the debris of limiting beliefs, the more you reveal your authentic self and the more your eyes are open to see others for who they really are, one with God and seeing people in the present moment without judgments as to where they are in life.

Up to this point, you likely bought into the stories you told yourself about how the world works. You allowed that unconscious programming to dictate your experience of the world until it matched the stories you were told. Our stories about our world have shaped it into what we perceive. Now is the time to tell new stories! What you now have is an opportunity to introduce new ideas about what is possible for your life and for the whole world. You do this by surrendering outdated stories and releasing the thought patterns that shaped how you see your life and the world. Surrender your ideas, your plans, and your dreams because living in a higher frequency will bring about even grander dreams, superior plans, and more elaborate ideas.

By surrendering and releasing beliefs about how the world is, you achieve a deeper understanding of being truly limitless and you begin to experience your view of the world in a more positive way. By surrendering to this place of acceptance you can live free from even your own expectations. You can begin relaxing and trusting that life will unfold for the highest good of all.

You are the world as you are reflected in each person you see. Everything is connected, we are all one. If one struggles we all struggle. What we resist within ourselves, others and the world by being hyper-focused on the negative keeps those unpleasant patterns repeating. The wars we wage on everything from poverty to drugs only serves to create more of the conflict of what we don't want. Our resistance holds negative situations in place. Though society can contribute many beneficial situations to our network of beliefs, they also create unhelpful societal expectations encouraging limiting beliefs, in the form of misguided opinions about the world. By releasing the beliefs that have cemented a negative charge to your experience of the world you can begin to heal everyone.

Negative programing through group consciousness conditioned us to believe that we alone are not enough to heal something so vast as the world. You can no longer deny your effect on the world as you have now re-learned to align with your Higher Self. Your Higher Self is where the magic of your inner knowing ultimately comes from.

A world without limiting beliefs releases us all from a system programed to disempower us. We simply need to make room for the idea that the world can become limitless.

Beliefs on limiting beliefs about the world you can clear:

I resist being a part of the world.

I resist making a move towards a life that excites me for fear I will lose what I have.

I resist the idea that I don't have to fight against what I don't want.

I resist trusting that the world's drug problem can heal itself.

I resist trusting that world hunger can be easily solved.

We all have to fight against what we do not want.

We all have to ban together to fight against all that is wrong with the world.

It is not possible to have a world without limiting beliefs.

I will never know a life that is free from limiting beliefs.

It's not possible to clear all my limiting beliefs.

There are too many limiting beliefs in the world to clear them all.

Limiting beliefs are just a part of life.

I need to have limiting beliefs in order to live.

If I clear too many limiting beliefs, I will no longer recognize myself.

The world needs to have limiting beliefs in order to have structure.

People need limiting beliefs in order to have structure.

The stories I tell myself about the world are true even if they are limiting.

We are made up of limiting beliefs.

I will keep obtaining limiting beliefs.

A world free of limiting beliefs has never been done before.

I cannot imagine a world without limiting beliefs.

I cannot imagine my life without limiting beliefs.

Finding all of my limiting beliefs is too much work.

Clearing the world of limiting beliefs is too much work.

I am just one person, there is no way for me to be able to heal the world of limiting beliefs.

The world as we know it might end unless we have limiting beliefs.

Too many people are too screwed up to heal.

The stories I tell myself about how people really are are true!

I wouldn't know what to do with myself if I had no more limiting beliefs to clear.

It is impossible to clear all the limiting beliefs I have about the world.

I can't live my truth because I may get judged by the world.

It is impossible to clear the world of limiting beliefs because there are just too many.

People will not be willing to do belief work for themselves to free the world from limiting beliefs.

People have fragile minds and freeing them from limiting beliefs would break them.

It's not enough for only me to get clear.

A world without limiting beliefs is only a fairy tale not possible or tangible.

It is not safe for me to be limitless.

It's not safe for the world to be limitless.

Living without limits makes me uncomfortable.

Without limits I won't know what to expect.

There are limits to my abilities.

There are limits to what I can do.

There are limits to what I can achieve.

There are limits to what I can heal from.

There are limits to what I can overcome.

There have to be limits.

I am limited by my own imagination.

The world is falling apart.

The world is crumbling around us.

The world is harsh, uncaring and dark.

There is no good in the world.

The world is nothing but chaos.

The world is fragile.

The world has already been destroyed.

There is no hope for a better, happier world.

The world is too broken to fix.

People are too obtuse to find common ground.

There is no common ground.

Everything is polarized.

Chaos rules the world.

You can't trust anyone in today's world.

I don't trust that the world will accept my authentic self.

I am afraid if I reveal my authentic self to the world it will demand too much from me.

The world demands too much from me.

There is only struggle, death and sadness everywhere you look in the world today.

The world is sick.

The world is unforgiving.

The world is hostile.

The future of the world is bleak.

There is no hope for a bright future.

World leaders have ruined everything.

World leaders are to blame.

Someone has to take the fall for the dark state the world is in.

Someone has to be blamed for all that we see is wrong with the world.

World leaders can't be trusted.

World leaders have taken all the power.

The world is a dangerous place.

It's not safe to be out in the world.

There is no balance in the world.

I view the world as dangerous.

I view the world as unstable and unsafe.

I can't find my place in the world.

I don't have a place in the world.

The world rejects me.

My talents and ideas have no place in the world.

I chose not to participate in the world.

I have closed myself off from the world.

I have to protect myself and the people I love from the darkness in the world.

All I see is how horrible everything is.

All I hear is how horrible everything is.

There is never any good news.

I must watch the news to be informed.

The news is the truth.

I believe all that the news reports.

The news has all the facts.

There is destruction everywhere.

There is devastation everywhere.

There is hate and death in all the headlines.

I see only hate in the world.

I only see neediness and laziness in the world.

I only see blame and entitlement in the world.

I see only corruption and dishonesty in the world.

I see only personal agendas and lies from world leaders.

I see only oppression in the world.

I see only apathy in the world.

I see a world where nobody thinks for themselves.

I see a world where nobody can do for themselves.

My environment has taught me that the world is an uncaring place.

There are too many problems to ever fix.

There are too many people who want things to stay the same.

There are too many world beliefs to clear.

Belief affirmations to free your mind and to allow for the possibility of a world free from limiting beliefs:

I am free to imagine a world without limiting beliefs.

I am free to accept a world without limiting beliefs.

It is possible for the world to be free from poverty.

It is possible for the world to be free from disease.

It is possible for the world to be free from limits.

It is possible for the world to be free from drugs.

It is possible for the world to be free from human trafficking.

It is possible for the world to be free from violence.

It is possible for the world to be free from intolerance.

It is possible for the world to be free from apathy.

It is possible for the world to be free from negativity.

It is possible for the world to be free from hate.

It is possible for the world to be free from abuse.

I can fully accept a life without limits.

I can fully accept that as I heal the world is healed.

I am free to imagine a life that is free of limiting beliefs.

It's ok to be myself, there will never be anyone else like me.

I love freely because it is part of being alive and human.

I live freely.

I am free to be my authentic self.

I can be and do anything I imagine.

I can imagine big and wonderful things for my life.

My limitless life is exciting.

My limitless life serves as an example for others to follow.

The joy I feel from being truly unlimited is a beacon for others.

I love just allowing my life to flow without my former resistance.

I am able to think and dream bigger than ever before.

Things change in an instant for the better.

I completely accept there are no boundaries to my experiences.

Great and wonderful things can happen quickly.

I accept a life that is greater than I can imagine.

I trust that I can imagine a greater life for me.

I experience the world as healthy and vibrant.

It is possible to live a life free from all societal expectations and to live life just for myself.

It's possible that everyone I meet can also live without limiting beliefs.

I trust that I am living a life free from limiting beliefs.

I trust that all the world is living a life free from limiting beliefs.

I see the world as free from limits.

I see my life as free from limits.

I trust that everyone can live a life free from limiting beliefs.

I can trust that the world can be free from limiting beliefs.

Clearing myself helps heal the world.

The more I clear the clearer my life becomes.

The more I clear, the more clarity I see myself.

The more I clear, the more clarity I see others.

The more I clear, the clearer I see the world.

The world is limitless, all things are possible in it.

I can imagine a healthy, vibrant world where everyone can be happy and fulfilled.

All that is for me to do is allow myself to imagine new patterns for the world to operate from.

Beliefs that hinder your ability to surrender:

Surrendering takes away all of my power.

Surrendering to others gives them power over me.

Surrendering to a higher power is impossible for me.

Only I know what is best.

Surrendering means giving up.

Surrendering means I have no way of doing something for myself.

Surrendering will take away all of my control.

I have to stay in complete control over my experiences.

Surrendering my expectations leaves me open for disappointment.

I resist surrendering.

I will not surrender.

I will never surrender.

I do NOT surrender.

It's not normal for me to live a life of surrender.

Completely surrendering my dreams is not something I am willing to do.

Completely surrendering my plans for my life is not something I am willing to do.

My expectations are important.

My expectations mean something.

It's foolish to surrender.

Surrendering means to give up.

If I surrender people will think that I am giving up.

The concept of surrendering is a lot of nonsense.

My surrendering will have no impact on the world as a whole.

I am afraid to surrender what I have worked hard to achieve.

I am afraid to believe that surrendering will help me.

I am afraid to surrender my own ideas of how my life should go.

Surrendering my habitual ways of being is too hard for me.

Surrendering to the unknown is terrifying for me.

I should not have to surrender anything.

Surrendering is useless.

Surrendering is just a lofty ideal with no basis in reality.

My truth is that even if I were to surrender nothing would change.

Surrendering means that I have no control over anything.

The world will still be a horrible place even if I surrender.

I will never clear enough limiting beliefs to bring me to the point that I am able to surrender.

I have too much baggage to surrender completely.

I have too much pain to surrender completely.

I am too broken to surrender completely.

I have too much doubt to surrender completely.

Positive belief affirmations to help you surrender:

By surrendering to God I am completely trusting that my life is is more fulfilling than I ever could have imagined on my own.

God knows better that I do.

I deeply and completely surrender to a higher power.

It is safe for me to surrender.

The more I surrender the more I allow life to open up.

The more I surrender the more I can allow others to be who they are.

By surrendering I show faith.

I am ready to surrender my old life in order to live a life that is in alignment with my authentic self.

I surrender the need to know how things will show up in my life.

I surrender the need to know how my life will unfold.

I understand that surrendering is the best way of having a life of freedom.

Surrendering equals freedom.

By surrendering I am free.

I surrender all attachments to how things ought to go.

Surrendering makes me clearer than ever before.

The more I surrender the more the world as whole heals.

Surrendering in each moment makes me stronger.

Surrendering brings clarity and peace to my life.

I am a master at the art of surrendering.

The Universe has a better plan for my life, all that is required is for me to surrender which I do with ease.

By surrendering I lead by example.

I surrender my anger, rage, and hostility towards the world.

I surrender my anger, rage, and hostility towards all others.

I surrender my anger, rage, and hostility towards myself.

I welcome the ease and patience that comes with surrendering.

All issues in the world will work themselves out by surrendering.

I surrender to God's idea of the world.

I surrender to God's idea of my life.

I surrender to God's idea of who I am.

I know what it feels like to surrender my need to control my environment.

I know what it feels like to surrender my life to a life free from limiting beliefs.

I know what it feels like to surrender my thoughts to the mind of spirit.

I know what it feels like to surrender my annoyance and anger about myself and the world.

I know what it feels like to surrender my lack of trust.

I know what it feels like to surrender my fear of people exposing my past.

I know what it feels like to surrender all my self limiting rules that are no longer serving me.

I know what it feels like to release all forms of mental control and fall into allowing and trust.

I know what it feels like to surrender all forms of mental resistance and fall into a state of allowing.

I surrender to the highest forms of love.

I rid myself of all the rules and barriers that are preventing me from surrender entering into my life.

I surrender to full potential.

I surrender to the love that is all around me.

I surrender my need to be right.

I surrender my need to be perfect.

I surrender my need to punish imperfection in others.

I surrender my need to punish myself for the imperfections I see in myself.

I surrender my need to do everything myself.

I surrender my need to be in control.

I surrender my need to protect myself by keeping others and the world at arms length.

I surrender my desire to suffer as a way to punish myself for my imperfections.

I surrender my fears of failure and of success.

I surrender my healing to God.

I surrender other peoples healing to God.

I surrender all those plans that did not work out.

I surrender all the sadness and pain I have held so tightly to.

I surrender all the baggage I have drug around with me for too many years.

I surrender my grief for all the losses I have perceived to have suffered.

I surrender my need to be flawless in the eyes of others and of the world.

I surrender to my highest good.

My physical body surrenders to its highest good.

My mental body surrenders to its highest good.

My ego surrenders to the highest good.

The collective ego of the world surrenders to the highest good for all.

Limiting beliefs preventing you from releasing:

I have to hold tight to the idea I have of who I am.

I have to hold tight to the idea I have of how the world is or I won't know how to navigate in it.

I am holding on to this idea of how the world sees me and I am not ready to let it go.

I am fearful of losing myself and all I have worked for by releasing.

If I release I lose.

Releasing is giving up.

Releasing rigidity is too challenging for me.

Releasing is too painful.

Releasing would make me face things I don't want to see.

Releasing would make me deal with things I don't want to even think about.

I am afraid to release my anger, it's the only thing that drives me.

I am afraid to release my blocks, boundaries and walls, as I need them to feel safe.

I need the stories I tell myself to survive.

Letting go is not something I am good at.

Letting go is not something I am willing to do.

Letting go means to lose on purpose.

I am afraid to release the old identity of myself which I perceive as truth.

I am afraid to release my attachment to past behavior.

I am afraid to release my outdated thinking.

Familiar limiting thoughts are a comfort to me.

I am afraid to release my outdated beliefs because they anchor me in the familiar.

I won't know who I am if I release the stories I told myself about me.

I don't think I can handle letting go.

Letting go is not safe.

Letting go is not enough.

I am too weak to release my limiting thoughts.

I need my blocks, barriers and walls in order to be safe.

I need my routines and patterns in order to make sense of the world.

I can't handle the world not being what thought it was.

I can't see new, healthy possibilities for myself, others, or the world.

I could not handle it, if life was easy.

I could never believe that the world can release all limiting beliefs.

It's not possible to release all limiting beliefs.

There are too many other people with ideas about the world to ever heal it.

My outdated stories about the world has value.

My outdated stories about myself have value.

My outdated stories about others has value.

The world is what it is.

People are what they are.

Positive belief affirmations to allow you to release:

I am ready to release all of my tired ways of thinking.

My limiting thoughts are no longer a comfort to me.

I release myself from the boundaries of my former behavior.

I am ready to open to the new ways of being in the world that are ready to emerge.

I release my struggle to God.

I release my attachment to the way I thought my life needed to go.

I release all attachment to my outdated programming.

I release all attachment to my stories about life.

I release all attachment to what was my life to make room for the abundance and joy waiting to manifest for me.

I release all attachment to the person I thought I needed to be.

I release all attachment to merely surviving to allow myself to thrive.

I release my attachment to the stories I told myself about every relationship I have.

I release all attachment to the blocks, boundaries and walls that I thought I needed to be safe.

I release my attachment to the past and all that has been in favor of living in the present.

I release myself from all future worries.

I release all of the rigidity I once had towards how the world is.

I release the need to control how my life happens.

I surrender my need to control how my life happens

I release the need to know how everything will happen.

I release my life to God.

I release myself and others from the boundaries I once had in place regarding all things.

I release everyone from my expectations for how I believe they should live.

I completely release all stress from my body and spirit now.

I completely release all worry from my mind now.

I release any residue left behind by my emotions of lower frequencies.

I release any residue left behind by the beliefs of lower frequencies.

I release all resistance to feeling and dealing with emotions.

I release all resistance towards allowing a bigger, grander life for myself.

I release all limiting beliefs from the world.

I release the energy of every limited belief I once shared with the world.

The world has been released from all of my past limiting beliefs.

I see the world as ready to release the energy that is causing past wounds to fester.

I see the world as ready to release all outdated stories.

I know every time I release an outdated belief the world is healed more and more.

I release all that I was.

I release all the outdated stories I told myself about what my life would become.

I release all outdated stories about who I thought I was.

I release all outdated stories about the motivations of others.

I release all outdated stories about how life is.

I release all outdated stories about how certain people are.

I release all outdated stories about the state of the world.

I release all that I thought I could be in favor of allowing God's vision of what I can be to take shape.

I release all blocks and barriers to an open heart.

My heart releases all the pain it has held on to.

My heart releases all the memories of pain from past circumstances.

My heart releases all blocks and barriers to love.

My heart releases its need to keep people away.

My ego releases all limiting ways it has designed to protect me from future hurt.

I release all blocks to an open mind.

I release all blocks to allowing.

I release all blocks to a more fulfilling life.

I release all blocks to completely loving and accepting myself.

I release all blocks to seeing the truth in every situation.

I release all blocks to reaching for a better, more empowering life.

I release my need to do everything for myself.

I release having to go it alone.

I release having to appear to be perfect.

I release feeling like asking for help is a sign that I am weak.

I release the feeling that I just want this life to be over.

I release all sense of hopelessness.

I release my grip on having a ultra tough exterior to protect me from others and the world.

I allow my body to release all discord and disease.

I release my attachment to the drama.

I release my attachment to all power and control in order to align to a higher power.

I release my attachment to the importance I feel in my job.

I release myself from the stories I allow to play out about the behavior of others.

I release my need to control the behavior of others.

I release myself from the stories I tell myself about needing to be employed by someone else in order to have security.

I release my attachment to my current job.

I release my attachment to my identity as a business professional. (Insert your own.)

I release my attachment to the titles that I have defined myself by.

I release my attachment to the the people in my current job.

I release my attachment to the stories I tell myself about what a perfect relationship looks like.

I release all habits of feeling like I will be in trouble for everything.

I release all thoughts that I am in trouble all the time.

I release all need to punish myself by setting myself up to be in trouble.

I release all need to punish myself for making mistakes.

I release all need to punish others for making mistakes.

I release myself from all limiting societal beliefs.

I release myself from all limiting inherited beliefs.

I release myself from the residue of all core limiting beliefs.

I release all resistance.

I release all that no longer serves me.

I release myself from the mask I have worn to hide my authentic self.

I release myself from the mask I have worn to protect myself from others and the world.

I release myself from all extra weight carried by my body as a way to protect myself from others and the world.

I release myself from all all rigid expectations.

I release my mind from the cloudiness that prevents me from finishing my project.

I release my mind from the cloudiness that prevents me from seeing the truth of my being.

I release the world from all blocks and limitations.

I release myself from seeing the world in negative ways.

I release myself from experiencing the world in any other way than positive and supportive.

I release all blocks to seeing and feeling my connection to God.

I release all blocks to seeing and feeling my connection to others and the world.

I release the world from all blocks to seeing and feeling a connection to God.

Journaling to solidify what you have learned.

By experiencing life with an open heart, we are able to view the world with ideas of what is possible. By clearing beliefs about others and the world what possibilities exist for you that were once blocked from your view?

_____

_____

_____

_____

_____

_____

_____

Surrendering is the fastest way to a life filled with joy, purpose, and abundance. Take time over the next several weeks to reflect on how surrendering has opened doors for you.

_____

_____

_____

_____

_____

_____

_____

When you become ready to release your past and all limiting identities you believed you were, it can temporarily leave a void. This void can be a bit uncomfortable as you may struggle to relate to the new self that is emerging. In the following space, create your own belief statements to both clear and replace with positive beliefs to make this transformation easier for you.

_____

_____

_____

_____

_____

_____

_____

SUMMING IT UP

This book was born from our journey to push beyond the boundaries our own limiting beliefs had created.

This book is also our gift to you as a part of helping everyone else who has unintentionally blocked their path and buried their authentic self underneath outdated and restricting beliefs. Because beliefs hinder so many areas of life, we are developing future workbooks that you will be able to use to clear other limiting beliefs surrounding your relationships, career, money, health and spiritual wellbeing. We want to help you find freedom in those areas by clearing beliefs so that you can change at the deepest level. We encourage you to continue clearing limiting beliefs for yourself. Start with setting aside five minutes every day to quiet your mind. Schedule an appointment with yourself—and keep it!

After many years of doing belief clearing, we can both testify to being in far better places than either of us would have ever imagined. We know that you will be filled with the same wonder and sense of discovery that we have both experienced. Once you begin, so much of your life will expand. So, here's to you, may your journey to freedom be filled with success!

ENDNOTES

Thie, John and Matthew Thie, Touch for Health: A Practical Guide to Natural Health With Acupressure Touch. California, DeVorss & Company, 2005.

Nelson, Bradley B. The Emotion Code: How to Release Your Trapped Emotions for Abundant Health, Love and Happiness. Nevada, Wellness Unmasked Inc., 2007.

Hawkins, David R. Power vs Force. Hay House Inc. 1995

https://www.amazon.com/Power-Force-David-Hawkins-Ph-D/dp/1401945074/ref=sr_1_1?ie=UTF8&qid=1531586957&sr=8-1&keywords=power+versus+force+by+david+hawkins&dpID=41SVLEI7bbL&preST=_SY291_BO1,204,203,200_QL40_&dpSrc=srch

Hay, Louis, You can Heal Your life. Hay House 1984

https://www.amazon.com/You-Can-Heal-Your-Life/dp/0937611018/ref=sr_1_1_twi_pap_1?ie=UTF8&qid=1531587344&sr=8-1&keywords=louise+hayes+you+can+heal+your+life&dpI

D=51kWvDjFGUL&preST=_SY291_BO1,204,203,200_QL40_
&dpSrc=srch

Brennan, Barbara Ann, Hands Of Light: A Guide to Healing Through the Human Energy Field. New York, Bantam Books, 1988.

ABOUT THE AUTHORS

Mayline Robertson grew up in the beautiful mountains of Montana. From a young age she maintained a constant interest in learning about health and healing the body. A life of skiing, horseback-riding and other outdoor pursuits took a physical toll on her body, and along with multiple major health with allergy challenges, led her at age 17 to visit a local kinesiologist who used Touch for Health techniques that brought immediate relief. That dramatic turnaround led her on a path to becoming a world-renowned kinesiologist and energy healer.

By her mid-twenties, Mayline had a degree in kinesiology and certification in Touch for Health and many other healing modalities. She applies these healing methods to balancing the body as a whole and to addressing more than just the physical body to bring about deep healing. Recognizing that spiritual and emotional healing are equally important, Mayline became certified in Spiritual Response Therapy. Combining several healing modalities, she now sees many clients in person and virtually as well as from North America, Europe, Asia and elsewhere. That experience and her openness to trying new techniques helped her realize how limiting beliefs were directly impacting those who had multiple health imbalances. They became blocked when certain emotions, which had been triggered by specific limiting beliefs, caused imbalances within the body. She found that those limiting beliefs held in a person's subconscious needed to be cleared away before true physical and emotional healing could happen.

Through the use of her intuition, kinesiology techniques, and several other healing modalities, Mayline has developed a simple system that allows people to find energy blockages in the form of limiting beliefs within the subconscious. She has learned to recognize the potential that each person has within as they travel at their own pace on their journey toward healing. Despite the many years Mayline has been practicing, she still finds great joy in seeing her clients grow and become their best selves, and she is excited to share the techniques for releasing limiting beliefs with all who read this book. Mayline travels between Billings, Montana, Florida, Massachusetts and Houston, Texas, to see clients.

A MESSAGE FROM MAYLINE

Using belief work as a tool in my practice has exponentially increased healing for many and allowed them to become more aware of how their thoughts impact their lives physically. Healing is taking place on so many levels within a session; however, the real healing is never done by my hands alone. I am only ever the vessel and the Channel for the highest vibrations of love in a client that I can connect with. Truly, that is where all healing emanates from, from within a person's soul and spirit when they allow their energy to come forth. Our guides and angels also assist whenever they are called upon in moments of need. My only hope is to help to bring each person to a higher consciousness of themselves and a true knowingness of their own personal connection to Source and to their Higher Self. It is an awesome task to do what I love to do every day and to be able to incorporate belief work into my practice.

NICOLE

Nicole Biondich was surrounded by energy work and healing from an early age. Her grandfather ran his own school of massage therapy and served as a massage therapist for over 50 years. He also mastered other healing modalities and imparted all that he learned to his family, especially to Nicole, who was close to him. Together they worked on a few his clients, each using the tools of their trade until a fuller healing could occur.

Always curious to better her life and herself, she studied all the healing and energy work concepts she could. Rooting out and pouring over every self help book she could get her hands on. It was however, through the work of clearing beliefs that Nicole really began to see her life change. The more she opened up to this new approach and the concept of limiting beliefs the easier life became. As part of her journey to uncovering hundreds of beliefs that limited her, Nicole developed the Inner Child meditation (described in chapter three) to help uncover, and finally break through to discover her authentic self.

This self-discovery and healing process became especially important as Nicole began to accept and explore her special intuitive gifts as a medium. Nicole's amazing and uncanny ability to channel messages had existed since childhood, but only by clearing beliefs was she able to let go of the limitations that had kept her from working openly as a channel for others. Since then, she has delivered many profound messages from clients' loved ones.

Having been friends with Mayline for years, Nicole began working beside her doing duel healing sessions of both the physical body as well as channeling spirit. Often in these sessions the limiting beliefs of client's came up to be healed. They discovered that they had separately been developing lists of limiting beliefs as well as writing what would become the book you now hold for more than a year. Astonishingly, when they combined their work into an early version of this book, there were no duplicated beliefs. This discovery confirmed that they should join their knowledge into a workbook that would allow others around the world to heal themselves.

Nicole lives with her husband Michael in Billings, Montana where she sees clients in person as well as meeting with clients virtually.

A MESSAGE FROM NICOLE

When I first began my journey to better health, I thought I simply had a bad case of allergies that had worsened to the point that it had affected my vision. After a few attempts of healing myself and several visits to Mayline, I directed my path to better health after realizing my illnesses were mainly rooted in core negative beliefs that were affecting the cellular structures in my body. Realizing this fact did not lessen the physical pain I felt, it just meant that the treatment needed for my body was not a pill, supplements, or an adjustment. The treatment needed to go much deeper. Sessions with Mayline, and a yearlong Miracles Coaching program developed by Joe Vitale, Introduced me to the idea of clearing not just emotions, but limiting beliefs. From then on it became a journey of writing down my own limiting beliefs, doing clearing work on them, capturing new beliefs that came up.

This was just one of many challenges during my journey that helped prepare me to co-author this book. Despite the difficulties, it allowed me to create a brand new life full of freedom and a feeling of self-appreciation that I had never known before. Now I live life as my true authentic self, in harmony with the work that I believe is my calling, being a medium, a healer, and writer. All things that just a few short years ago I could only imagine. Every challenging step of this process was worth how wonderful I feel today.

Using belief work has helped me to heal from every negative situation in my life and to move forward in ways never imagined. The process of clearing ingrained beliefs within the core regarding biased judgments and other stubborn ideas is no easy task, but I can attest that the end results and relief are dramatic and life changing. It is my greatest hope that this work will give you the power to take back your life as much as it continues to empower my own.

Lightning Source UK Ltd.
Milton Keynes UK
UKHW010308080223
416649UK00009B/237/J